HOW TO FIND THE PERFECT JOB IN 30 DAYS OR LESS

How to Find the Perfect Job in 30 days or less

Fast, easy tips and proven techniques
to find a great job fast

by Paul Fontaine

Writers Club Press

San Jose New York Lincoln Shanghai

How to Find the Perfect Job in 30 days or less
Fast, easy tips and proven techniques to find a great job fast

Writers Club Press
an imprint of iUniverse, Inc.

For information address:
iUniverse, Inc.
5220 S. 16th St., Suite 200
Lincoln, NE 68512
www.iuniverse.com

ISBN: 0-595-24525-0

Printed in the United States of America

Contents

Introduction

Finding a job can be a great experience but also a challenging one. You are at a crossroad right now where opportunities are all around. Very rarely do you have this type of chance to positively affect your life. I will give you the necessary tools to help you find your perfect job. This ebook will guide you as you write your cover letters, resumes, and thank you notes. It will also be with you when you walk into your interview and then negotiate a great job offer.

This book is written by someone who has had success in finding the perfect job. Me! The perspective of this book is from the job hunter's point of view. Many job search books are written by Human Resource professionals or Executive Recruiters who spend all of their time on the other side of the desk. I will show you what has been successful for me and for many others.

Here's what I ask of you:

1. Use this book. Go to the links. Sign up for services. The beauty of this book is that it is interactive.

2. Read and re-read this book. Even if you only have time to re-read certain sections, you'll find information here that will help you be successful not only in finding a job, but also in life.

3. Set goals. Always write down your goals and review them often. This is one of the keys to a successful life.

I've made mistakes and learned from them. I have hired good employees, but also bad ones. I have received good, and not so good, job offers. My intention for this book is to help you to succeed in finding your perfect job.

This book is divided into six chapters. Each chapter is a separate stage in finding your perfect job.

Listed below are the six stages:

1. Setting objectives and getting organized.

2. Creating resumes and cover letters that get you an interview.

3. Searching for job opportunities online.

4. Preparing for your interview and following-up.

5. Negotiating the best job offer and accepting.

6. Solidifying future success in all of your career endeavors.

Whether you are unemployed, looking for a career change or just curious about the job market, start your new life today. This is your chance to find your perfect job. The following are the secrets, tips, and know-how you need to it. Now, let's get down to business.

1

Set Your Objective and Get Organized

Let's get motivated

If you are not employed at this time, treat this job search as your new job. Each day you need to get up around the same time you used to get up for your 9 to 5 job and get started. It takes some discipline, but you can do it!

Studies show that people who consistently devote time each day job searching tend to find jobs sooner than their counterparts. If you are fortunate to be currently employed and you're looking to make a change, you will need the same discipline to work evenings and weekends while you search.

It's time to begin. I will walk you through the process from setting your goals for the perfect job to searching, interviewing and finally accepting! Let's start with focusing on what you want. It's hard to achieve something if you are not clear as to what you want. Here's the question of the day: **What is your dream job?**

As with anything you want to do, you need to first figure out exactly what it is you want to achieve. Are you looking for your first job out of college? Have you been out of the job market for a few years and need to get back in? Are you looking to change careers? Are you unemployed and need a job fast?

Whatever your situation, there is an answer. When you begin looking for a job, take the first day, or even just half the day, to figure out what is your perfect job. Do you want a part-time job? Something close to your home (if so, how close: walking distance, 15-minute car ride, etc)? Write down how much you want to earn, what size company you want to work for and if you want benefits such as healthcare.

> *"Laziness may appear attractive, but work gives satisfaction."*
> *Anne Frank*

Describe what characteristics your next job or career will have. Where should it be? Is it in a company or are you interested in working from home? Focus on what you <u>really</u> want and be specific. This is your chance to do something you've always wanted to do, so don't confine yourself to writing down characteristics of jobs you've had in the past. Focus instead on what you really want for the future. Write down the **Job Search Objective** now. It doesn't need to be more than a sentence or two.

Here are a few Job Search Objectives to help you get started:

- Find a full-time teaching position at a high school within 45-minute drive

- Change careers by obtaining an entry-level position in a large advertising agency in Boston

- Work in a Sales Management role in a growing high technology company within the state

- Accept a part-time office manager position in my town

As you can see, each of these examples states the general location of where the person wants to work and also describes specifics about the position and the company. The more details you put in your objective, the easier it is for your mind to focus on exactly what you are trying to achieve. Once your mind targets the goal, it's difficult to stray from it and that's what you want!

> TIP: You can also use your Job Search Objective (or a modified version) as your Objective Statement on your resume. We will discuss this topic later in Chapter 2, but keep this in mind.

What if I'm not sure what type of job I want?

If you are struggling with what you really want, there are a few websites that can help you determine what type of careers or industries best suit you. The most well-known include the Myers Briggs test which you can take at **www.discoveryourpersonality.com** and the Keirsey Temperament Sorter and Keirsey Temperament tests. You can click on **www.keirsey.com** and take a test to help you understand your temperament and personality.

Also, the Occupational Outlook Handbook is a great resource and can be found at **www.bls.gov/oco/home.htm.** Then you can sit down and craft your Job Objective.

> *"Imagination is more important than knowledge."*
> *Albert Einstein*

Offline, I recommend *What Color is your Parachute?* 2002 by Richard Nelson Bolles. This book has been in circulation for years and has helped me, along with millions of others to define their mission in life and to find the career that is best for them.

James C Gonvea, President and CEO of Gonyea and Associates Inc., states in his recent article, *Ten Jobs to Watch in 2002*, that the best areas in the near future for jobs are:

• Healthcare

• Information Technology

- Specialty areas

He goes on to say, "The healthcare and computer fields are still hot, as technology continues to improve and the Baby Boomer generation begins to retire. And some professional positions that require specialized skills are also expected to see growth. According to the US Bureau of Labor Statistics, job postings in these industries are expected to grow anywhere from 40 percent to 100 percent in the next few years."

Some of the positions James emphasizes are:

- Database Administrators

- Paralegals

- Correctional Officers

- Home Health Aides

I encourage you to investigate different jobs and industries. Speak to people who are already working in the type of job that interests you. Ask them what they like and dislike about their job and what personal qualities one needs in order to succeed. We will talk about informational interviews later in this book, but this is one method of learning and researching which type of job you may enjoy.

I know what I want to do, but I don't have the qualifications.

If you believe that your dream job is difficult to obtain because you don't have the necessary experience or education, then take steps to change the situation. Only you have the power to begin again and start fresh.

Some ways of attaining the knowledge or experience needed for a new job or career are by taking a course or attending a seminar. It doesn't have to be affiliated with a college, nor does it need to be at a degree-granting institution. There are many businesses, online and offline, that offer courses on computer programming, healthcare services, administrative skills, and accounting to name a few.

Some organizations offer free seminars and courses, such as **www.blackboard.com** and **www.free-ed.net**. Available options include receiving certification in a certain area of expertise or simply taking a few courses in a specific concentration, such as word processing or web design.

> *"Nobody can be successful unless he loves his work."*
> *David Sarnoff*

Many of the web designers I have worked with online have taught themselves or just taken a one-day course. Don't let lack of experience keep you down. The money you spend on a seminar or class will pay for itself in the first year of your new job.

Another useful way of getting experience is through volunteering. A business may not pay you to learn new skills, but a non-profit organization is more willing to give you a chance. Volunteering can help you gain experience in many aspects of business such as fundraising, office management, leadership, communications, direct marketing and more.

As an added bonus, you can "give back" to a cause you believe in by volunteering with your favorite non-profit organization. I have learned a great deal through volunteering and have used much of that experience to clinch some of my best jobs.

Some people get into a rut where they have been working in the same field for many years and now feel trapped. They are making good money in their current profession, yet their passions are somewhere else. Sometimes you need to take a pay cut in order to gain the experience you need to change your career. It's a tough pill to swallow, but it will be much better in the long run. Life is too short to not enjoy your job.

Job search overview

Now that you have thought about your perfect job, written it down (I urge you to write it down, it will work wonders for you, trust me), and shared it with someone close to you, it's time to begin the job search. There are many methods for finding a job. Listed are some of the major channels:

- Online job sites and corporate sites

- Networking

- Classified ads in papers

- Ads in trade magazines

- Job boards/Job posting

- Recruiters (headhunters)

- Employment agencies

- College alumni associations/Career centers

Each method has its good and bad points, and some will be discussed here. Much of Chapter 3 concentrates on the online portion of the search, but remember that this is only one of several productive ways to find a job. I urge you to explore all of the above channels in order to maximize your job search.

It's all about networking

Networking, still today, accounts for many of the jobs filled. Even if you don't see yourself as one of those people with a big Rolodex containing hundreds of business cards, networking is well worth your time. Networking simply means communicating with people. You can call, email, fax, whatever way you want. If you haven't been networking in the past, make sure you start networking immediately.

An easy way to begin networking is to make a list of at least 15 people you have worked with previously or anyone who you think might be helpful in finding you a job. You'll be surprised how many people you know who will be helpful. You may not see the results immediately, but as the saying goes we're all separated by only "six degrees."

In 1967, Stanley Milgram, a psychologist, coined a phrase "small world phenomenon," after producing one of his creative experiments. His findings proved that you could connect any person in the U.S. with anyone else by only associating, at most, six other people. Hence the "six degrees of separation" phenomenon.

It's the old Kevin Bacon game where someone selects a celebrity's name and you have to connect Kevin Bacon to that person by naming six people or less.

Here are examples of job connections I have seen people make:

- After sharing his career goals with friends, this job hunter found out that his best friend's co-worker now owned a business in his desired field. After some initial calls, the job hunter flew to Chicago for a full day of interviews

- A informational phone interview is scheduled after someone sees an email address in a friend's mass email with the name of the company where she wants to get a job

- Sitting at the same table with a Senior Vice President during a wedding leads to a job interview two years later

So my point is, whatever the situation, when applying for a position, it's always better to have a positive connection at a company.

Compare the two cover letter excerpts below:

Networking Positioning

"Mrs. Smith, the production manager, referred me to you as the best person to speak to regarding the manager position. Please see my attached resume for your review."

Traditional Positioning

"I am applying for the manager position. Attached is my resume for your consideration."

The second example doesn't stand out in the pile of cover letters. The first version is what makes you unique in the crowded job market. Every little bit helps and in this situation, the first person has a much better chance of being called in for an interview.

Almost 75% of jobs obtained come from networking. It's never too late to start building your network pool. The #1 rule to follow is: don't "burn bridges." Hans H. Chen, a writer for **www.vault.com**, in a recent article entitled *Don't Burn Employee Bridges: Exit Interviews and Alumni Network,* states "An employee who quits his job can always choose between a graceful exit and a blazing discharge of long-suppressed dissatisfaction...."

It is extremely important, in both the short and long-term, that you utilize every experience to make your next career step a smooth and positive one. Everytime you leave a job, layoff someone, or submit your resignation, think about this rule. It may be difficult at times, but in the long run, you'll be happy you followed it.

There are many places you can network. You can network at parties, through volunteering, sporting events, and even supermarkets. Any time you are in the presence of people, you have an opportunity to make a new career contact. It takes a little bit of guts sometimes to step out of your comfort zone and approach people, but you'll be happy in the end that you took the chance.

Always follow-up conversations with the question "Do you know anyone in company X?" or "Is your company hiring? And if so, who is the best person for me to speak with?" Lastly, it is always appropriate to ask the person if he or she would mind if you use his/her name as a reference when speaking to the contact. Let's begin!

Set networking goals

The one thing I've learned in this market place is that you need to sell yourself 'cause no one else is gonna do it. It's up to you. Each day you can choose to move forward and take a few steps toward your perfect job or you can sit back and hope someone calls you. The people who choose to move forward are the ones who will be working at their new job in the next 30 days.

Set goals for yourself. For example, decide that you will call three people each day or that you will send out fifteen resumes per week. Again, write those goals down on the same sheet that you used for your Job Search Objective. This will be your **Job Goal Sheet.**

Type it up in big letters. Tape it on your wall or put it up next to your computer, wherever, just make sure you see it and read it numerous times a day. The Job Goal Sheet is what you want, in your words, no one else's. The more you read it and take action, the better your chances of getting that call for your perfect job.

Below is an example of a Job Goal Sheet:

Job search objective: To obtain a manager position in a large, well known direct marketing company located in New York City.

Job goals:

1. Send 3-5 resumes out to potential employers each day

2. Call at least 2 contacts per day to set up informational interviews or actual job interviews

3. Send a follow-up email to companies 2 weeks after sending resume/cover letter

4. Schedule at least 3 interviews within the first 2 weeks

Below is a blank Job Goal Sheet for you to write in your personal information:

Job Search Objective:

_____

_____

_____

Job Goals:

1. _____

2. _____

3. _____

4. _____

Let other people help you out: The role of recruiters

There's no need to search for a job all by yourself. As you've probably been told many times, you can accomplish more as a team than you can by yourself. For some people, recruiters are a beneficial part of the job search. How helpful a recruiter will be depends on what type of position you are looking for and what experience you have.

Recruiters tend to be more useful the higher you are in the "food-chain." Some manager positions are available through recruiters, but more likely the positions will be Director/VP and above. It's okay if you are not at that stage. It's something to look forward to if that's one of your goals.

There are many executive recruiters and most specialize in different fields and industries. I will list a few major ones for you in Chapter 3, but in general it is best to go to a search engine such as **www. google.com** and type in "recruiter" or "headhunter."

The Internet's vast reach in finding the perfect job

Online job sites have become a major factor in the job search industry. Currently, there are nearly 50,000 websites devoted to job searches and careers. There are a few major job search sites such as **www. monster.com**, **www.hotjobs.com** and **www.ajb.dni.us** (America's job bank) that account for many of the jobs advertised online.

Not only can you apply for jobs at these sites, but you can also post your resume for potential employers to view. This is a new aspect of the job search that was not readily available before the Internet. I have found that posting my resume has been quite fruitful. You will be surprised how many employers and recruiters utilize this aspect of job websites.

There are different levels of privacy with online resume databases. The one with the least amount of privacy is an open database that allows anyone online to access and view your resume. On the other end of the spectrum, there are databases where you control who can view your resume. You assign a password, which is needed in order to gain access to your information. There are also databases that only show your experience and do not show your personal information such as name and address.

Of course, there are always drawbacks to posting your resume. If you are currently employed and want to keep your job search confidential, you may not want to post your resume for everyone to see. There are options on most job posting sites where you choose the levels of privacy you want, and exclude certain companies from possibly seeing your resume.

You never know where your resume may end up once you post it online, so be careful. You may think you are only posting your resume to one job site, but in reality, over the next month or so, it could be sent to many other places due to the beauty of viral marketing (when people send or forward information to other people, it becomes a "spider web" touching many points).

There are general job search sites as well as specialized ones depending on what field you're looking for or what type of job you want (i.e. adventure job, part-time or freelance). Listed in Chapter 3 are the some of the largest and what I believe are the "good" and "not so good" websites out there. Each has its pros and cons; I will leave it up to you to decide which is best for your search.

As with anything relating to the Internet, website names may change or posted links may not work. I will do my best to keep this book up to date. If you find any that don't work, please let me know at **info@EasyOnlineGuides.com**.

Good ol' fashion Sunday paper classifieds and alma maters

As always, newspaper and trade magazine classified advertisements need to be on your list of places to concentrate on. Depending on the position, some opportunities may still only be advertised offline in local papers, for example.

Some job seekers find success in utilizing their college career centers. Go to your alma mater and use their placement services. It's a known fact that people tend to hire employees who are like themselves. There is a bond between fellow alumni. Take advantage of it.

CHAPTER 1—SUMMARY

- **Set your Job Objective**

  Spend your first day brainstorming and writing down a detailed description of what type of job you want.

- **Ways to find out what you want and how to get it**

  Websites such as **www.discoveryourpersonality.com** and **www.keirsey.com** can assist you in learning about yourself and what jobs may best suit you. If you know what kind of job you want, but don't have the needed experience to get it, consider volunteer opportunities to acquire the skills. Additional education is a valuable chance to add a balance to your previous work experience.

- **Job Search Overview**

  There are many methods you can utilize to find your perfect job. In the chapter we review online job sites, networking, classified ads, recruiters and more.

- **Networking**

  Networking still accounts for the majority of jobs filled. Networking simply means communicating with people. If you haven't been networking in the past, it is important you begin as soon as possible. Some good places to network are through friends and past work associates. In addition, take advantage of opportunities at your church or in social gatherings to find out about potential job openings that may appeal to you.

2

Resumes and cover letters that get you interviews

The most important document of your search—Your resume

The main purpose of a resume is to get you an interview. Your resume is a sales document. You are acting as a salesperson when you are sending out your resume. This section will concentrate on creating the most effective sales tools (i.e. resume and cover letter) to successfully land those important interviews.

The Rules of Resume Writing

- Must be easy to read.

- Use concise phrases and action verbs.

- Be specific with achievements. Quantify by using numbers. Keep it specific.

- Think about each word and edit out any words that do not contribute to your message.

- Use the same words that the employer chose in the advertisement.

- Take a few extra minutes to understand the company's business and tailor your resume to the company.

- Proofread. Have your partner or friend review it. The more eyes, the better.

Resumes Formats

Resumes, in general, come in two formats:

1. **Chronological**: In this type of resume, your most recent experience for each category (i.e., education or work experience) is listed first, with earlier ones listed after that. This is the most commonly used format and the format of choice by most employers. I recommend using this format for the majority of readers.

2. **Functional**: If you are a recent graduate or are returning to the workforce after a long time period of not working, you may opt for a functional resume. This format concentrates more on the skills you have acquired and not necessarily the positions you have held. If you acquired computer skills, such as web page design while volunteering, you can highlight these skills upfront on your resume. If your most recent position has nothing to do with the job you are applying for, you may want use a functional format.

The following are good samples of both, chronological and functional resumes **(Keep in mind all resume samples are shown in larger font so they can be easily read in this book. Resumes should, in general, be 1-2 pages).**

Chronological formatted resume #1

Jason C. Wallach
1340 10th St • Washington, DC 20015
555-555-1212 • **jasonw@usa.com**

EDUCATION

GEORGE UNIVERSITY, School of Business   **Washington, DC**

Master of Business Administration   *May 2002*

- First place winner of 2000 Challenge Business Plan Competition with clinical trial patient recruitment business.

- First place winner of 2001 mobile commerce feasibility study competition.

- Co-President, George Entrepreneurs Association; Vice-President, IdeaChallenge business plan competition.

- Research Assistantship to co-write article on how clinical research organizations expedite the drug approval process.

DUKE UNIVERSITY   **Durham, NC**

Bachelor of Arts with Honors: Art History/Pre-Medicine   *May 1993*

PROFESSIONAL EXPERIENCE

PBR ASSOCIATES   **Washington, DC**

Summer Associate, Health Care Practice   *June–August 2001*

- Provided clinical trial operations expertise and designed integration plan for a Health Care Systems during its acquisition of a contract research organization.

- Conducted gap analysis, documented process flow maps, and presented operational improvements to the Health Care Systems' clinical research pre-award and post-award office.

Chronological formatted resume #1 (Continued)

CLINICAL RESEARCH   Philadelphia, PA
COMMUNICATIONS

Associate Director, Strategic Data   *September 1998–July 2000*
Operations

- Designed and implemented strategies for 15 biopharmaceutical clients, which decreased the time necessary to introduce new drugs to the market by 3 months and significantly improved research quality. Supervised 35 clinical and data personnel to accomplish these new strategies.

- Supervised the management of data quality and database collection technologies, which reduced average project costs by over $450K and the time to completion by approximately 1 month.

- Evaluated the individual contributions of 15 employees within the Strategic Data Operations Department and implemented a reorganization plan that improved morale, increased productivity by 20%, and improved employee retention by 50% within the team.

- Ensured repeat business of $3M in six months by strengthening client satisfaction.

Senior Project Manager, Clinical Data Management

- Increased annual revenues by 25% from previous year through management of 7 project teams. Provided on-time and below budget delivery of 19 clinical trial databases. Presented clinical database strategies at over 40 client meetings.

- Streamlined budgets, resources, and timelines resulting in annual savings of $750K.

- Developed and implemented company's Internet patient recruitment product.

Chronological formatted resume #1 (Continued)

SOURCE, INC.	**Newtown, PA**
Account Service Consultant	*November 1996–August 1998*

- Directed consulting team for $4M contract with Bristol Inc. to help optimize sales and marketing efforts, maintain margins, and maximize profits. Co-authored proposal for five-year $12M renewal of contract.

- Designed and implemented strategies for daily market share reporting to increase sales of top performing cholesterol drug.

MPS, INC.	**Philadelphia, PA**
Data Manager	*June 1993–October 1996*

- Supervised staff of 20 clinical and data personnel in national project with the Social Security Administration (SSA) to provide treatment strategies to recipients of Supplemental Security Income.

- Co-designed operations concerning data collection and processing, quality assurance, and database maintenance.

ENTREPRENEURIAL EXPERIENCE

- Co-founded Wellness website, a B2B provider of proprietary wellness and complementary medicine content.

- Self-Employed Artist—Exhibited and published painter and photographer. Sold over 35 works to private collectors and corporations.

Author's Comments:

This resume emphasizes the education portion of this candidate's experience. He recently completed his M.B.A. and since that will qualify him for higher level positions, he chose to feature that on top of the resume. His accomplishments are clear, measurable and specific. At the end there are a few unique aspects that help him "stand out" in the crowded job market.

Chronological formatted resume #2

Elizabeth C. Payne

Cellular 555-555-1212	10 Main Street
Home 555-555-1000	Baltimore, MD 21010
elizpayne@usa.com	

Objective

A challenging leadership position in which I can apply my experience in marketing, strategic management consulting, program development, and project management.

Major Clients

American Express	AT&T Wireless	Chase Manhattan Bank
Cingular Wireless	Citibank	First USA Bank

Experience

Director of Teleservices and Client Account   April 2001 to Present

DeKlein International   Alexandria, VA

Chronological formatted resume #2 (Continued)

Responsible for the overall direction and management of the Teleservices and Account Management Departments. Direct all Teleservices marketing functions including Training Design, Development and Delivery, Quality Assurance, Sales Verification, Scripting and Performance Enhancement. Oversee the Client Account Management team responsible for growth of our marketing efforts in both telemarketing and direct mail. Responsible for the development and execution of new client business and new product strategy in the telemarketing and direct mail channels. Negotiate both client and vendor contracts. Routinely participate in due diligence conducted by potential clients. Attend client strategy meetings and explore additional revenue opportunities with clients. Travel internationally and domestically for vendor site visits and audits on a regular basis.

- Increased revenue in the Teleservices Department from $71,000/month to $800,000/month. Moved from last place to the 2nd largest revenue channel in less than 9 months.

- Increased overall sales performance by over 800% and decreased vendor costs by 28%.

- Decreased the cost per sale from $120.81 to $9.49.

- Increased new client accounts by 300% and introduced 6 additional products in the telemarketing channel.

- Streamlined the procedures for new business startup to execute new programs in less than 2 weeks compared to a previous 4-6 week execution.

Senior Program Manager   October 1998 to March 2001

Marketing Direct, Inc.   Vienna, VA

Provided expert on-site process business and telemanagement consulting services to our call center partners. Reviewed, evaluated and developed processes for the quality assurance and training departments. Identified gaps in procedures and recommended solutions for performance enhancement. Managed program budgets and projections by achieving client objectives such as cost per sale, or hour commitments, and by reviewing all client and vendor invoices. Responsible for the overall direction, coordination and evaluation of a staff of four. Developed program specific startup documents, scripts and training materials for direct marketing programs. Recommended, identified and conducted program training as necessary. Oversaw lead management and reporting requests for client. Negotiated both client and vendor contracts.

Chronological formatted resume #2 (Continued)

Senior Consultant/Senior Program Manager	October 1997 to October 1998
TMM Enterprises	Alexandria, VA

Routinely conducted due diligence on prospective vendors. Attended client meetings and developed presentations as required. Maximized relationships with clients & vendors to ensure quality & performance objectives of the contract were met.

- Hand selected by the SVP as part of a small team providing on-site process business and telemanagement consulting services to Enron resulting in the successful launch of The NewPower Company.

- Designed, developed and implemented a Quality Assurance certification program for new agents under tight deadlines.

- Led the sales skills training classes that increased sales conversion by 95% in one week.

- Managed revenues of $25 million per year in telemarketing efforts for credit card acquisition, membership service, LD, and cellular.

- Awarded Employee of the Quarter October–December 1999.

Marketing Manager	January 1996 to October 1997
Framin Bank, Inc.	Chevy Chase, MD

Created and coordinated 29 separate direct mail offers, which ran simultaneously. Ensured correct print production and inventory control. Assisted with the daily coordination between the direct mail agency and the database processing company. Supervised the scheduling and delivery of tapes, reports, and data transmissions. Audited and approved information in each transmission to assure the integrity of the data.

Site Coordinator	March 1991 to November 1995
First Bank, Inc.	Wilmington, DE

Managed and maintained a UNIX based predictive autodialer for Collections Department. Managed staff of 4 Production Flow Coordinators. Responsible for all production flow reporting. Responsible for all downtime management and tracking of all 4 call centers throughout the country. Reduced past due accounts from 6% to 5% in 9 months.

Chronological formatted resume #2 (Continued)

Education

B.S., Business Administration   May 1990
University of Delaware   Newark, DE
Concentration: Marketing

Professional Associations

Member, NAFE—*National Association of Female Executives*

Author's Comments:

This format is very easy to read and the separate sections are clear. The lines between each section create a professional look and enhance the organization of the resume. This person has elected to utilize an objective. As you can see, the objective is broad enough as to not knock her out of the running for being too specific. Emphasizing her work experience first is the right strategy for her and ending with her professional association affiliations adds uniqueness.

Chronological formatted resume #3

BARBARA M. PETERMAN
2353 American Avenue
Philadelphia, PA 90358
555-555-1000
bpeterman@usa.net

SUMMARY

Project manager experienced in restructuring websites, conducting usability studies and developing editorial content. Primary liaison with clients, business partners and interdepartmental teams. Organized problem solver and skilled team leader capable of managing multiple, concurrent projects in fast-paced environment.

WORK EXPERIENCE

CAMBRIDGE DESIGN, INC.   Philadelphia, PA   2000-present

Senior Information Architect/Usability Specialist

- Evaluate and restructure websites for clients including associations and governmental agencies.

- Manage website projects through entire development process and create workflow scenarios

- Conduct usability studies and audience interviews with users and stakeholders; perform heuristic and contextual analysis

- Organize and repurpose content to adapt for web use

DISTRICT UNIVERSITY   Washington, DC   2002

Adjunct Faculty, Internet Studies

Chronological formatted resume #3 (Continued)

- Taught Information Architecture course as part of Web Development and Web Content Producer certificate programs

- Provided students with skills needed to effectively structure web content

- Taught systematic process for developing, evaluating, and testing user-focused websites

SOCIETY PUBLISHING   Washington, DC   2001

Picture Editor, Non-Fiction Book Division

- Selected all photographs and artwork for historical biography

- Researched archives and image collections to find many rarely-seen images

- Determined picture outline for entire book in consultation with team members

- Negotiated payments, permissions and usage rights

KID'S LIFE BOOKS   Alexandria, VA   1987-2000

Project Editor

- Identified new business and partnership opportunities; monitored industry and marketplace trends

- Managed editorial process from conceptualization through all stages of market research (focus groups and surveys) to product launch

- Developed content for history, science, health, home improvement, gardening and lifestyle categories

- Determined schedules and budgets for projects averaging $4MM each

Chronological formatted resume #3 (Continued)

Design Director/Art Director

- Designed and produced award-winning illustrated reference books

- Managed $350K art and design budget per year; negotiated payments and contracts

- Supervised design department staff and freelancers

- Coordinated workflow between departments; ensured quality during all stages of production

PROFESSIONAL COURSES

Computer Communications and Training   Alexandria, VA

> Information Design for the Web
> Internet Marketing
> Project Management for Web Development and Publications

Washington University   Washington, DC

> Finance and Accounting
> Publications Management

District University   Washington, DC

> Information Architecture for the Web

EDUCATION

Rhode Island School	Providence, RI	1982–1985
Bachelor of Arts Degree, Graphic Design		
Montreal University	Montreal, Quebec	1981–1982

AWARDS

American Art Institute, AAI	1996
Kid's Life Books, Above and Beyond Award	1998, 1997, 1996

Chronological formatted resume #3 (Continued)

<u>COMPUTER SKILLS</u>

Adobe Acrobat, HTML, MS Word, QuarkXpress

<u>PROFESSIONAL MEMBERSHIPS</u>

American Society for Information Science and Technology
DC Information Architects

Author's Comments

This person has over 15 years work experience so she opts to begin with a summary section. This is a great way to concisely state who she is and what she has to offer to a potential employer. Her accomplishments and duties are action-oriented, utilizing words such as "manage" and "organize." The latter half of the resume emphasizes additional training, awards, skills and professional affiliations. This section could be shortened a bit, but the overall strategy is a good one.

Functional resume

BRENDA STILLMAN
234 S. Main Street
Anywhere, USA 55555
(401) 555-1212
Brenda@usa.com

OBJECTIVE

To find an office manager position.

SUMMARY OF QUALIFICATIONS

- Six years experience as Office Assistant at fast paced consulting firm.
- Proficiency in MS Office and Quickbooks, along with Powerpoint and Excel.
- Strong organizational skills and attention to detail.

RELEVANT SKILLS

Administrative Assistance

- Supervised administrative assistant.
- Wrote minutes for meetings and added information into the database.

Payroll Management

- Handled bookkeeping for 13-person office.
- In charge of accounts payable and receivable.

Functional resume (Continued)

Customer Service

- Researched and responded to over 10 customer complaints per week.

- Handled face-to-face contacts on daily basis with major clients.

WORK HISTORY

| 1991-98 | NOW Associates | Office Assistant |
| 1986-90 | ABC Trucking Co. | Administrative Assistant |

EDUCATION

| Katharine Gibbs School, Providence, RI—Administration Studies | 1985 |
| Smithfield High School, Smithfield, RI—G.P.A. 3.2 | 1984 |

Author Comments:

Brenda has a gap in her employment history from 1998 to present. While this was a personal choice, there is a need to de-emphasize this aspect and emphasize her skills and qualifications. Brenda may also want to consider addressing this gap in her cover letter or, at the very least, be prepared to answer questions about it during her interview (but since there are never guarantees that she'll get an interview, I'd recommend addressing any gaps in the cover letter). A broad objective statement is a good choice here since her resume may not tell the right story to a potential employer.

Best practices for cover letters

Prior to an interview, resumes and cover letters are your main communication and sales tool for a potential employer. Nowadays, the resume is significantly more important than the cover letter. I'd say at least 75% of an employer's time is spent reviewing the resume and only 25% or less on the cover letter.

Some experts I spoke with while conducting research for this book stated that they rarely review cover letters. I still believe a cover letter has a place in the job search, it is just that its significance has changed.

Cover letters should be short and to the point, especially when included in the body of an email. Ten years ago, cover letters were a full page or two detailing specific accomplishments, but this is no longer the case.

> TIP: If you want to be certain the person reviewing your resume finds out specific information, make sure it's on your resume. Don't "save" a few accomplishments for your cover letter! If it's not in the resume, the majority of the people may never see it.

Below are examples of cover letters, each tailored to the specific situation.

Cover letter/email #1

Dear Ms. Petro:

I am very interested in the assistant manager job posted March 22nd on **Monster.com**. Below is a summary of my qualifications:

- Three years experience as a coordinator in the same industry.

- Bachelor's degree in management with a minor in communications.

- An ability to absorb information quickly and put that learning to use.

I look forward to speaking with you soon regarding this position. Below, I have added my resume to the body of this email.

Sincerely,

Neil Page
(555) 555-1000

(paste resume here)

Author's Comments:

This cover letter format is good for choosing 3-4 specific points from the job description that you want to emphasize quickly and clearly to the reviewer.

IMPORTANT: In addition to using the same words in your cover letter/resume as the employer used in the advertisement, another good format for the cover letter is taking three or four main points of the job description and comparing them to your experience.

For example:

JOB DESCRIPTION STATES	YOUR COVER LETTER STATES
5+ supervisory experience	"With over 8 years experience supervising..."
At least 2 years day care management	"I have managed a day care center for over 6 years"
Ability to work in team environment	"In my previous two positions, I worked in teams of 3-6 people in order to accomplish our goals."

Cover letter/email #2

Dear Sir/Madam:

I am writing to inquire about the position of Director, Product Line Marketing. I believe with my publishing background and 10 years direct marketing experience in large companies, I can greatly assist your company in achieving the goals set forth in this position.

Everything I do is with passion. Each employee that works for me and every associate I work with receives encouragement, thought-provoking questions and every piece of knowledge I have to succeed. In addition, my ability to effectively lead a team and build businesses has been proven over and over in each of my positions.

I look forward to speaking with you about this exciting opportunity. Have a good day.

Please see accompanying resume.

Sincerely,
John B. Smithfield
(555) 555-1000

(paste resume here)

Author's Comments:

This is a short and sweet version to utilize in general situations for people who are more comfortable writing out sentences rather than pulling out specific points.

Cover letter #3

Dear Sir/Madam:

I am writing to inquire about the Loan Processor position. I am very interested in being considered for this position, since the requirements are commensurate with my experience and career interests. I am relocating back to the Boston area in the first week of April and will be available to begin employment immediately thereafter.

I have extensive experience in processing loan applications from receipt to closing. My diverse background shows a pattern of growth in companies and increased responsibility within the banking and loan industry. My five years of proven results, along with my strong attention to detail will assist me in significantly adding value to your company.

Please see attached resume. I look forward to speaking with you.

Sincerely,
Mary Wyatt
(555) 555-1000

(paste resume here)

Author's Comments:

This cover letter is good for individuals looking to relocate or needing a few extra lines to describe their work scenario. The resume is not the place to describe any out-of-the-ordinary work situations, such as relocation or career changes. The cover letter is the more appropriate communication tool to briefly discuss your situation.

TIP: Look for key words or skills listed in the job description. Be sure to state clearly in your cover letter that you possess those skills (if in fact you do). It will not only show the reviewer that you are a match for the job, but also that you actually took the time to read the job description carefully.

Best practices for resumes

Spend the time upfront to create a general resume with a solid foundation. That way, once a general resume is created, it won't take you long to tailor it to each specific job opportunity. From my experience, a one or two-page resume is enough for almost everyone. If you have to go to three pages, you probably haven't spent enough time choosing the most concise statements or you may have gone back more than 15 years of your past experience.

In general, the most relevant information and experience occurred over the past 10-15 years. Anything prior to that time period becomes significantly less relevant. If you did a one-year stint with a public relations firm twenty years ago, unless it is extremely relevant to the position you are applying to, don't include it as part of your resume.

> *"Don't go around saying the world owes you a living. The world owes you nothing. It was here first."*
> *Mark Twain*

When writing your resume, continually ask yourself if the reader would be interested in what you are writing. If the job is for a very specific programming position and you have past experience in IT and also non-profit fundraising, you probably don't need to relay the latter part on your resume.

Put yourself in the other person's shoes and ask, "If I was the one hiring for this position, is this information relevant to the job advertised?" Instead of adding a few lines about your fundraising experience, take a few extra lines to add one of your past programming positions to emphasize what you accomplished. Also, if your education is more than 15 years old, you might want to drop the year graduated.

> **TIP:** Try to include something unique on your resume as a talking point. You need to make people remember you.

To elaborate on the tip above, I went to school and lived in China for a few months in the 1990s. I can't tell you how many people during an interview ask me about this particular detail. It's a little thing like this that makes people remember you when it comes down to choosing the person for the job.

Another friend of mine speaks Portuguese and has this as one of his skills at the end of his resume. He has also said that many people are impressed and ask him about this aspect when interviewing, even if they aren't specifically looking for someone with this skill.

While this may seem to contradict what I previously said about deleting any information that may not be relevant to your job, this one personal, unique trait has a purpose. You can't get hired if they don't remember you. After many interviews, people just meld into one group.

Resumes have many possible sections and how you choose to format your resume depends upon your personal experience. The majority of resumes will have the traditional **Work Experience** and **Education** sections. In addition, some remaining sections include:

- Objective statement

- Summary of qualifications

- Volunteer activities, interests.

- Achievements

- Professional associations

- Skills/certifications

If you are just out of school and lacking work experience, you should emphasize your education and may want to add sections on volunteer activities and general achievements.

If you are an established manager in the IT industry, you will probably want to describe the skills and certifications you received. Also, a summary of qualifications may be best for you since it will give the reader a chance to quickly pick out the key words and job requirements needed in the position.

Objective statements: To have or not to have?

There are differing opinions about having an objective statement in your resume. My opinion is if you are just out of college, or have less than 5-7 years work experience, it is probably best to have an objective statement. It shows a potential employer what you are looking for and confirms for them that what they are offering is in line with what you're looking for in a position.

Plus, if you are new to the job market you usually have a problem filling up space on a resume due to lack of experience, so an objective adds a good, formatting balance to the resume. The #1 problem with objectives is people either make them too specific or they make careless mistakes when deciding what to write. You don't want to get yourself knocked out of the review process because of either of those problems.

In his article, *Some Resume Objectives Do More Harm Than Good*, Robert Half approaches the topic with a bit of humor by looking at some job objectives that may have backfired for the applicants.

"OBJECTIVE: To work for a company with a warm environment and great pay."
Our thermostat's always set at 72 degrees. As for the pay...

"OBJECTIVE: To utilize my skills and experience working for an aggressive company, but more important, a well-balanced company."
We walk a tightrope every day.

"OBJECTIVE: To work as a bookkeeper where acuracy is appreciated."
Accuracy is always appreciated here.

"OBJECTIVE: To utilize my profound ability to analyze or sense a finanical condition or situation that..."
Finanical conditions are always tough to...spell.

Robert goes on to state, "Personally, I feel this category should be omitted. While including an objective generally doesn't hurt a candidate's chances, writing one that's too narrow will prompt a hiring authority to judge your credentials and potential only against that specific objective."

Here is an example of an objective that is too specific:

Objective: To find a director position in a large steel manufacturing company where I can utilize my skills in industrial engineering and also in product development.

Overall, it's great to know exactly what you want and I urge you to write this down for yourself (on your Job Goal Sheet), but do not write this on your resume for a potential employer to see unless the objective matches exactly to the job description.

In the previous example, what happens if you apply to a company that is not in the **steel** industry? Maybe it's a **small** steel company and not a **large** one, or the job doesn't entail **product development**, just **engineering**. How about if it's a **manager** position and not at **director** level? All of these are opportunities for potential employers to decide that what you're looking for isn't what they have to offer.

A better objective might be:

Objective: A challenging position in the manufacturing industry that will give me the opportunity to increase my skills and grow with the company.

If you are looking to change careers, an objective statement may more effectively communicate your desired career path. After you have been around the job market for awhile, objectives take on less significance. You may be better off taking up that precious "real estate" space by adding more details about your positions or skills.

If you are going to write a specific objective, make sure it matches the exact job for which you are applying. In general, the advice to keep your objective broad comes out of the need to resolve the problem of people not targeting their communications to each employer (which unfortunately happens often).

By all means, write a specific objective statement, as long as you tailor it to the job description. If you are sending out numerous resumes without targeting the objective than you are better off keeping it more broadly focused.

The who, what and how of electronic resumes

In the new world of online job searching, creating an electronic resume is essential. An eResume is simply formatting your present resume so that the employer can open the file and read it clearly. In order to create your eResume, you will need to save your resume as plain text or text only (also called ASCII). For the sake of simplicity, I will use the term plain text.

Plain text is an appropriate term because that's exactly the outcome you will receive when you save your resume in this file format. There will be no boldface type, no underlining, no bullets or italics. Also, I recommend using a regular font such as Arial or Times New Roman to ensure readability from both humans and machines.

> **TIP: Email a copy of your plain text resume to yourself and a few friends first to see how it looks in different email programs before sending it out.**

More and more companies are scanning resumes in order to put them into a database and search for applicants based on keywords. To ensure that your resume is scannable, get rid of the following:

• Bold print

• Underlining

• Bullets

• Italics

• Tabbed format

• Out-of-the-ordinary fonts

Instead of using bullets, you can use asterisks for plain text resumes. Since you are not able to bold face words to make them stand out on your resume, try using all CAPS for sections such as EXPERIENCE and EDUCATION.

You should keep two versions of your resume: a scan-friendly eResume and a traditionally formatted resume with bullets and tabs, etc. If you are applying to a Fortune 500 company, chances are they will be using resume-tracking systems. If it's a smaller company, the chances are less that they will use tracking software, but you never know.

You need to find out what format the employer prefers. To be safe stick with a plain text resume when you use email to apply for a position. You can always follow-up with a nicely formatted hard-copy version of your resume if you desire.

What's the best way to send your resume and cover letter?

As you see from the graph on the following page, email has become a mainstay in business communication. Some experts say that you should not attach your resume and cover letter to an email. Others say it's acceptable. My recommendation is to do exactly what the job posting states. Many job postings state the preferred method of resume delivery. If by chance it does not or you are sending an unsolicited resume, I would cut and paste your plain text resume contents into the body of your email.

The other option, which can work best at times, is to both paste your resume content into the body of the email as well as attach it for their convenience. The one drawback for this option is that you increase the possibility of the email getting deleted because it has an attachment. Some businesses automatically delete outside emails that have attachments for fear of viruses.

For the majority of your business correspondence, has e-mail replaced snail mail (i.e. traditional mail)?

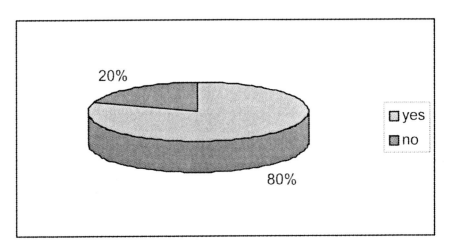

*Source: **Vault.com** E-mail Behavior in the Workplace Survey of 1,004 Employees, May 2000.*

Regarding offline searching, if you are going to fax your resume, I suggest following up with either an emailed resume or a traditional mailed resume. Faxes are still not the best option when it comes to readability and you never know how well it may reproduce.

When sending your information by email, if you are applying for an advertised position, place the job title in the subject line and any relevant job identification number. If you are sending a "cold resume" (when you are not applying to a specific advertisement or job posting) to a recruiter or contact person in a company, make sure the subject line is intriguing enough to get the recipient to open it.

For example:

Subj: Electrical Engineer Manager looking for new job opportunities
or
Subj: Direct Marketing Guru with MBA, resume enclosed.

8 biggest resume-writing mistakes:

1. Not targeting to the specific job.

2. Not having someone else, beside you, carefully proofread.

3. Not being concise. Going to too many pages, writing about an experience that is not relevant or too old to be significant. You need to be clear and concise so you can "walk" the reader through your experience.

4. Not being truthful. Many people may tweak their resume here and there to "expand upon" their experience, but that practice can and, most times, does backfire.

5. Not putting all of the important information in the resume. Some people pull one or two points out of the resume to discuss solely in the cover letter. Wrong.

6. Using your present employer's email address or work phone number as points of contact.

7. Not stating your accomplishments and achievements effectively. Be specific and use action verbs when describing your role at each company (i.e. managed, created). Quantify accomplishments (i.e. increased sale 50%, grew business by $100,000).

8. Not continually updating and editing your resume based upon feedback received from employers and recruiters.

> TIP: Whenever you are on the phone or in person with someone who is reviewing your resume, carefully listen to their questions and how they interpret your resume. Many of the questions they ask are key points you may want to clarify on your resume.

A few years ago, someone asked me about a past employer and what type of products it manufactured. I spend a lot of time detailing in my resume what I did in the position, but forgot to discuss the overall picture of the company's product lines or industry.

Remember, it is important to put yourself in the other person's shoes. Most companies are not well known, so you need to make sure the reader can easily understand what type of company it is and what you did there. You only have approximately 30 seconds before the person reviewing your resume makes a "keep or reject" decision. Make sure it's right.

The following are some good examples of resumes along with a before and after sample. Changes are made to the "before" resume in order to create a more effective communication tool for the applicant.

Before and After Resume:

Before Resume:

Samuel Hightower
16 Smith Street
Main Town,USA 99999
555-555-1000
Shightower@usa.com

OBJECTIVE: To pursue an Engineering Management position in a high tech company which utilizes my varied employment and educational background.

EDUCATION: **BOSTON UNIVERSITY**, Boston, MA
August 1996
Master of Business Administration in General Management
Courses in Leadership, Operation Management, Statistics, Negotiations, Entrepreneurship, Organizational Behavior, Market Research, Economics, Marketing, Accounting, and Finance.

WENTWORTH INSTITUTE OF TECHNOLOGY, Boston, MA
September 1988
Bachelor of Science in Mechanical Engineering Technology

COMMUNITY COLLEGE OF RHODE ISLAND, Warwick, RI
December 1989
Associate Degree in Engineering
Course emphasis in Electrical Engineering and Mechanical Engineering.

EXPERIENCE: **Extreme Circuits Inc.**, Cranston, RI
Assembly Engineering Manager (April 1997-Present)
Manage a group of engineers and technicians in all aspects of supporting five automated surface mount assembly lines during three shifts of operation, manufacturing flexible circuitry of polyester substrate, printed with conductive ink and silver epoxy solder.
Responsibilities included: Budget creation and maintenance, Hiring and assimilating new employees, Analysis of manufacturing data.

Before Resume: (Continued)

CIRCUMER CONNECTION SYSTEMS, Nashua, NH
Project Leader (January 1995–April 1997)
Supervise and manage all aspects in the creation and
release of specialty designed production equipment. This
includes design, develop and implement a multi-axis
computer controlled production spray machine and
pneumatic connector shear with programmable logic.

Packaging Engineer (December 1992–Jan 1995)
Fulfill customer packaging requirements as well as original
packaging systems and design. Developed new suppliers.
Initiated internal processes and methods to support quality
and shipments.

Manufacturing Engineer (October 1988–December 1992)
Responsible for assembly robotics, tool and equipment
design, as well as process analysis and development. Also
skilled in training and project management. Experience in JIT
& TQM. Macintosh, Unix and DOS/Windows experience.
AUTOCAD 12 proficient.

CTI CRYOGENICS Helix Technology, Waltham, MA
Production Engineer Assistant (September–December 1987)
Defined processes, investigated processing equipment,
detailed work cells, estimated and requisitioned equipment.
Tested and recommended components for new product.

ACTIVITIES: Skiing & Snowboarding, Home Brewing, Mountain Climbing,
SCUBA diving

Author's comments:

Overall, the example isn't bad, but the format and accomplishments
need to be clearer. See "After" version.

After Resume:

Samuel Hightower
16 Smith Street
Main Town,USA 99999
555-555-1000
Shightower@usa.com

OBJECTIVE

A Sales and Marketing Management role in a growing high technology company where my leadership ability to identify prospective customers, build relationships and close business deals will contribute to company growth.

EXECUTIVE SUMMARY

Accomplished, technically proficient Account Manager with over 10 years of experience in supporting customers. Adept in a diverse assortment of skills including identifying and developing new business, application engineering, segment marketing and executing product quotes

---

PROFESSIONAL EXPERIENCE

Extreme Circuits, Inc   **Cranston, RI**   **1997–Present**

A leading designer and manufacturer of polymer thick film flexible circuitry.

After Resume: (Continued)

Senior Account Manager   1999–Present

Provided sales support to diverse positions within a potential accounts, ranging from Management, Purchasing, and Program Management to Engineering. Targeted those needs by demonstrating the benefit of the product. Presented clear, useful information to facilitate the growth of the relationship including follow-up.
Result: Market sales growth from $4 to $6 million.

Created the foundation for the Telecommunication Marketing Plan. Researched and identified 25-30 target companies guided by the plan. Created a contact management system. Directed Sales Representatives to the targets, to explore potential opportunities. Worked in cooperation with them to develop the accounts.
Result: Awarded more than six new applications per month quoted, each with total revenue potential from $1 to $3 million.

Assembly Engineering Manager   1997-1999

Managed a department of engineers and engineering technicians in all aspects of supporting and improving five automated surface mount assembly lines and value-added manual operations during three shifts of operation

Conceptualized an image of a more efficient manufacturing operation, and implemented a product specific rate and yield benchmarking and monitoring system for all SMT circuits. Prioritized and managed resources to address and eliminate problem areas identified by the system.
Result: Improvements ranging from 7.5% to 220% increase in production rates. Product yields averaged above their goal 70% of the time in 1998.

Circumer Systems   Nashua, NH   1988–1997

Manufacturer and assembler of some of the world's largest and most complex PC boards, as well as an assortment of specialty connectors.

After Resume: (Continued)

Project Leader   *1995–1997*

Supervised and managed all aspects in the creation and release of specialty designed production equipment. Including designing, developing and implementing a multi-axis computer-controlled production spray machine and pneumatic connector shear with programmable logic.

Packaging Engineer   *1992–1995*

Fulfilled customer packaging requirements as well as design of original packaging systems. Developed new suppliers. Initiated internal processes and methods to support quality and shipments through packaging.

Manufacturing Engineer   *1988–1992*

Engineered assembly robotics, tool and equipment design, as well as process analysis and development. Skilled in training and project management with experience in JIT, FMEA & TQM.

EDUCATION

Boston University   **Boston, MA**   **1992**

M.B.A. General Management, Entrepreneurship Concentration
Leadership courses: market research, marketing, statistics, negotiations, organizational behavior, operations management, accounting and finance.

Wentworth Institute of   **Boston, MA**   **1988**
Technology

B.S. in Mechanical Engineering Technology
Course emphasis in Electrical and Mechanical Engineering

Author's Comments:

This format is clear and concise. Since this person has over 10 years experience, an executive summary has been added to give the reader a chance to quickly understand who this candidate is. Results-oriented bottom lines have been added to each position and quantified. The *Education* section has been placed after *Experience* which is the right decision in this situation since experience is more relevant to his objective than his degree.

There is another document I recommend creating for your interview. A "leave behind" detailed career summary. This document is a more detailed view of your achievements and experience. It takes on a similar format as your resume, yet it is printed on quality paper and is given to an employer at the end of the interview. Even if the employer does not read the career summary, you have stood out and showed how you go above and beyond the necessary requirements.

The next page is an example of a detailed career summary.

Samuel Hightower
16 Smith Street
Main Town,USA 99999
555-555-1000
Shightower@usa.com

OBJECTIVE

A Sales and Marketing Management role in a growing high technology company where my leadership ability to identify prospective customers, build relationships and close business will increase their sales, market share and company growth.

EXECUTIVE SUMMARY

Accomplished, technically proficient Account Manager with over 12 years of experience in supporting customers. Adept in a diverse assortment of skills ranging from developing new business, application engineering, segment marketing and executing product quotes. Utilizing these skills, results in expanded market position and customer relationships that achieve increased company growth and profitability.

PROFESSIONAL EXPERIENCE

Extreme Circuits Inc., Cranston, RI   **1997-Present**

A Division of Parlex Corporation

Sr. Account Manager   **1999-Present**

Developed a rapport with new and potential customers, while managing the on-going relationship with current customers. Account management for world-class customers in the telecommunications and computer peripheral industries, such as Ericsson, Lucent Technologies, Nortel Networks and Motorola. Duties included: inside and outside sales, market research, development of market plan, project management, quoting and costing as well as technical support to sales.

Assembly Engineering Manager   1997-1999

Managed a department of engineers and engineering technicians in all aspects of supporting and improving five automated surface mount assembly lines and value-added manual operations during three shifts of operation.

Circumer Systems Nashua, N   1988-1997

Manufacturer and assembler of some of the world's largest and most complex PC boards, as well as an assortment of specialty connectors. Customers range from the telecommunications industry to the military.

Project Leader   1995-1997

Supervised and managed all aspects in the creation and release of specialty designed production equipment. This includes designing, developing and • implementing a multi-axis computer-controlled production spray machine and pneumatic connector shear with programmable logic.

Packaging Engineer   1992-1995

Fulfilled customer packaging requirements as well as design of original packaging systems. Developed new suppliers. Initiated internal processes and methods to support quality and shipments through packaging.   •

Manufacturing Engineer   1988-1992

Engineered assembly robotics, tool and equipment design, as well as process analysis and development. Skilled in training and project management with experience in JIT, FMEA & TQM.

EDUCATION

Boston University　　　　　　　　　**Boston, MA　1996**

M.B.A. General Management
Leadership courses: market research, marketing, statistics, negotiations, entrepreneurship,
organizational behavior, operations management, economics, accounting and finance.

Wentworth Institute of Technology　　　　　**Boston, MA　1988**

B.S. in Mechanical Engineering Technology
Course emphasis in Electrical and Mechanical Engineering

SELECTED ACHIEVEMENTS

SALES

Developed and implemented a plan to grow sales in an existing market. Accepted assignment; researched, recorded and summarized market activity; defined the market; determined prospective products within the specified industry; identified active companies in the market; refined target list; researched market leaders; determine contacts; developed targeted sales presentation; conducted formal and informal seminars; promoted value of the product; gathered technical details; solved problems for client; oversaw design progress; quoted recommended solutions; closed prototype sale; facilitated manufacture of prototypes; participated in inside design reviews; coordinated component and material acquisition; participated in determining process steps; assisted transition of prototype to customer; work with cross-functional customer groups to resolve resultant design issues; aided in finalizing product definition; closed production tooling and volumes. **Result:** Market sales growth from $4,000,000 to $6,000,000 in two years.

Built relationships with decision-makers, ranging from purchasing, program management and engineering to facilitate the growth of relationship. Reviewed and checked weekly requirement reports; monitored manufacturing lead-times; discussed requirements with buyers; recommended placement of critical supply orders; translated requirements and progress to program managers; facilitated project evolution; provided information including follow-up to engineering; guided design and sustaining activities; provided options and suggestions. **Result:** Achieved an open partner-like relationship with the customer. Open communications insured design-in status by inclusion in the early stages of the new product development design cycle.

Established primary customer contact for over six strategic accounts. Awarded key account responsibility; managed daily account activity for multiple worldwide customers in the telecommunications and computer peripheral industries; initiated and led customer visits; presented company background and led technical discussions; educated customers of new technologies and developments built strong relationship with decision makers of each company: Understood their needs and implemented methods to accomplish them. **Result:** Received a prototype order for over $20,000 followed by a pilot run, with potential sales of over $2,000,000.

Established a methodology to conduct international sales calls. Visited new, current and prospective accounts to initiate sales growth; educated audience; listened to customer needs; achieved mutual understanding of benefit. **Result:** Achieved sole-source status by guiding the customer during the design-in phase, and built closer relationships.

MARKETING

Researched and identified 25-30 target companies; generated target list based upon company research; identified facility locations, list functions performed at each facility, engineering and purchasing contacts within target facilities, and specific products each location is responsible for; Created contact management system to track activity; worked with manufacturers representatives to develop accounts; directed sales representatives to targets, explored potential opportunities; made sales calls to target companies. **Result:** Achieved more than six new applications quoted per month. Total revenue potential of the opportunities is $1 to $3 million.

Initiated actions to broaden scope of present target markets. Researched new technology developments; identified possible growth opportunities; evaluated companies business strategy based upon research; demonstrated achievements; highlighting examples; established customizing to their requirements. **Results:** Developed relationships with over eight new customers, and received more than $500,000 of new sales

TECHNICAL

Solved problems in the role of sales engineer. Worked in cooperation with electrical, mechanical and component engineers to review and access the technical aspects of product being designed; provided guidelines and suggestions to develop the product for ease of manufacturing; improved efficiencies in manufacturing; explained intricacies of resulting design; established better understanding and comfort utilizing a different technology; accomplished in depth customer understanding of the technology facilitates; increased new product opportunities. **Result:** Over six new opportunities presented and quoted with potential sales of $2,000,000.

CHAPTER 2—SUMMARY

- The most important document in your job search is your resume. It's your sales tool.

- Resume format: chronological and functional. The majority of job applicants should utilize the chronological format.

- When writing cover letters keep them short and utilize key phrases from the job postings.

- Resumes need to be easy to read, organized clearly and proofread by different people. Resumes need to have specific achievements. Use measurable results to highlight achievements and keep it concise. Don't write broad statements.

- Whether you have an objective statement or not is your decision. If you are changing careers or just starting out, an effectively written objective statement can be beneficial. If you have been working for many years and are looking for a position in the same field, skip the objective statement and utilize that space to elaborate on your achievements.

- Save your electronic resume in plain text format and make sure it does not have any bold print, underlining, bullets or italics.

- Best method of sending your resume and cover letter: do whatever the job posting states. If it does not specifically state a method, copy and paste your plain text resume and/or cover letter in the body of an email. Many companies delete any emails from outside addresses that have attachments due to virus concerns.

3

The online job search...Let the games begin!

Keep organized in your job search.

Follow these steps when applying for jobs both, online and offline.

1. As soon as you send out a resume, print or cut out the job description.

2. Create a "to follow-up" folder and place the printed job description with the sent date in the folder.

3. Create a "followed-up" folder and place printed job descriptions with commentary on the back of the page or attached to the description of when you followed up and what are the next steps (see below for further information).

4. Create an "active folder" for any jobs where you have had a phone interview or actually went to the company for an interview.

5. Lastly, create a "archive folder" where you place all jobs that have been filled or jobs which you have followed up numerous times and have not heard back over the past 3 months.

I have found #3 above to be a key part of the online job search. Sometimes you will receive an automatic email reply back from an employer stating they received your information, but other times you are left wondering if your information was ever received. Because of this, I have always recommended sending a follow-up email 3-4 weeks after your initial email was sent to the employer.

An example of a follow-up job search email is below:

Dear (Name) or Sir/Madam:

Hello, my name is Paul Boland. I sent my resume to your company last month regarding the Construction Manager position. I wanted to follow-up to confirm that you received my information and also to find out if you have an update on the status of the position. Any information would be appreciated. For your convenience, I have inserted my resume below. Thank you for your time.

Paul Boland

(insert resume below)

I have found this step to be quite effective in getting a response. You may either get a response that the position has been filled or hopefully a response asking you to come in for an interview. This step acts as a reminder and also asks in a professional and casual manner for an answer.

Job searchers are often left wondering if the employer has even looked at their information. This step can confirm that someone has reviewed your information/resume—a much-appreciated aspect for weary job searchers who are having difficulty even getting a response from companies.

> **TIP:** Make a list or an Excel spreadsheet to store your website registration information such as user names and passwords. Take the sheet and staple it to the inside of your Job Search folder so it's easily accessible. Nothing delays finding jobs more than forgetting passwords or user names.

Resume sending services—Good or bad?

Many people have asked me about a service that has surfaced over the past couple of years that will email your resume to thousands of recruiters for a fee typically ranging from $40 to $95. I personally have not utilized this service, but the value of this service depends on the person. If you want to save time trying to find the recruiters that are in your specific industry, this service could be of use.

"Nothing will work unless you do"
Maya Angelou

A service such as **www.resumezapper.com** will email your resume and cover letter and do minor targeting to various locations. The bottom line is that a majority of recruiters will not be interested in your resume because they do not specialize in your field. Currently, most resume sending services distribute your information to thousands of recruiters, but probably only 5% of the resumes, at most, will be sent to the audience you need.

I spoke with a few recruiters about these services and in general they say the same thing: They learn how to pick out which emails are sent by these services and if the subject line doesn't call out to them, they just delete the email.

Ron Gregory, an executive recruiter who specializes in Direct Marketing, said that he opens the email if it has a subject like "DM Executive, MBA." If the subject line says "High-Tech Computer consultant resume attached," he deletes it because the resume is of no help to him in his job placements for direct marketing executives.

One of the main rules of resume and cover letter writing, and also of job searching, is that you must target your communication to the specific position and audience. Utilizing a service that distributes your resume and cover letter across the board will only send one, generic version. There are many other services you can use for free that can get your name out there such as job boards or sites with job posting sections.

For information regarding headhunters or to order the famous Directory of Executive Recruiters with over 5,200 search firms, please refer to the link. **www.kennedyinfo.com/er/corpder.html**

Job search website directory and reviews

As of this past year, according to the Fordyce Letter, "employers and recruiters use the Internet and the Web to make 48 percent of all their hires." There are close to 20,000 new jobs posted online each week. I'll show you how to find the ones that interest you.

Over 125 job websites are detailed in this chapter. To help you sort through these, we've evaluated and reviewed more than half of these sites. The following information was compiled to assist you in utilizing the Internet in the most effective and efficient manner possible.

TOP RECOMMENDED SITES

- America's job bank (**www.jobsearch.org**) or **www.ajb.dni.us:** This site is very in-depth and a great place to find state and government jobs. U.S. Department of Labor is the major force behind this site. It is easy to understand and navigate. Overall, we really liked the site. It has a good search engine that yielded accurate results. When we did a sample search for "accounting," the positions listed where actually for accounting rather than for account managers like other sites reviewed.

  Also, the quality of positions seemed better than most. There were not many temporary jobs or the ubiquitous "work at home and make millions" positions you see on a lot of sites. Most positions seemed to be traditional full-time positions.

- **www.careerbuilder.com:** One of the top job search sites. You can select from multiple states and job interest fields. The search is easy to understand and there are lots of fields to narrow your search. If you are searching multiple locations or job fields make sure you deselect "all locations" and "any" under job description because you'll get thousands of jobs…something they need to correct on the site.

  It is easy to apply for positions since most of the postings have an email address to send your resume. There is no need to register as a member and its reach is quite expansive since it searches over 30 job databases.

- **www.careerjournal.com:** This site is good for executives and middle managers brought to you by Wall Street Journal. We found a good quantity of jobs and effective search options. There are special, career reports offered along with a database on seminars and job clubs. While the job search is free, other aspects of the site require payment, but hey this is after all the Wall Street Journal! You pay for the reputation of high quality information and you get it here.

- **www.careerperfect.com:** While you can search for jobs and post your resume, this site is more of a resource in career planning, resume writing and finding out what type of job is best for you. Overall, very professional site with good information for finding out what job is best for you through career testing.

- **www.careerweb.com:** This site has a good search engine and an easy to sign up email notification when jobs come up in which you may be interested. Overall, it has a good amount of positions available. A sample search yielded: 558 IT positions nationwide, along with 204 in education and over 1,000 medical/healthcare.

  This site has an interesting component for people looking for office administration positions such as secretaries, data entry and office managers. You can instantly interview for office administration jobs online. The service is called Jobwire and it does not require a resume. Just answer a few questions and the information is forwarded to Office Administration employers in the area of your choice. If an employer is interested, they will call you.

  For some positions, the site takes actual advertisements printed in their weekly publication, The Employment Guide, and scans them, so when you click on "details" you see a graphical advertisement similar to what you would read in a magazine.

- **www.employment911.com:** You have to login and join to utilize the free services. A slightly painful experience due to the large amount of cross-selling and upselling of other services/products you have to go through, but overall it's worth it. Lots of jobs pulled from many job sites. Site states "over 3 million jobs from more than 350 job sites."

- **www.flipdog.com:** Interesting site that pulls in job postings from company sites. At time of review, it had approximately 450,000 jobs available. You have to be cautious at times because some postings may be old or obsolete, but overall it's a good site. Definitely sign up for the email job alerts.

- **www.headhunter.net:** Another major job search site, now affiliated with **careerbuilder.com**. Many positions available on this site. Easy search and lots of ways to break down the search. Your search results also display salaries for many of the positions, which is great.

  Site also ranks and prioritizes jobs by "Performance Posting Value,"—the amount of money employers and recruiters have paid to control the position of their jobs in the search results. Good for employers, slightly annoying for job searchers since most sites sort by recency of job posting.

- **www.hotjobs.com:** This is one of my favorite sites. You can select to view positions posted in just the past day; most sites force you to at least view the entire past week's postings which can be more time consuming. The search engine offers many ways to narrow the search. Make sure you sign up for the email service to send you targeted jobs of interest.

  Site has a printer-friendly feature that prints job descriptions so words and sentences aren't cut off like other "printer-unfriendly" job sites. One drawback is with the advanced search, you can only choose 1 state so this aspect is inefficient; many other sites offer options to choose several states simultaneously.

- **www.jobbankusa.com:** Job search engine is limited, but results were very detailed. Results showed salary ranges, if relocation would be offered, years of experience needed and posting dates. Overall quantity of positions was moderate compared to what we have seen with other sites. A lot of resources available regarding industry and career news.

- **www.jobsearchengine.com:** Amazing meta job search engine that searches over 250 American job boards. It's very fast. You'll see listings from Flipdog, JobsOnline, Headhunter, Yahoo and Wall Street Journal….and much more. Had a few glitches when trying to get details on jobs. Good place to go when you want a lot of results FAST.

- **www.monster.com:** This is one of my favorite sites. Over 1,000,000 job postings! Good search options. Easy set up to get email notification of jobs you may be interested in. Many international sites available. Over 3 million subscribers to their free e-newsletter. Site has specialized areas to help focus your search: ChiefMonster for higher income, executive-level positions; MonsterTrak for college students and recent grads; Hmonster for healthcare professionals. It goes on and on.

- **www.salary.com:** This is a well known and useful site for doing research on, yup, you guessed it, salaries. In the beginning this site was solely used by most to find out how much they were worth, but now it's a lot more. Job listings have been added. This site presently has over 100,000 listings.

  I've used this site's information as reference when requesting salary increases during annual review periods. The site has a very easy sign up for the email job agent to send you job posting emails at whatever interval you choose.

- **www.topechelon.com:** Easy search options and one of the best listing formats I've seen. The format includes a summary of 10 jobs on the left side of the screen and then it gives the details of the first job listed on the right side. Lots of information such as salary, date posted, years of experience needed. Very nice and fast. You do have to register to reply to jobs, though, and the form is a bit long.

- **www.vault.com:** Great site. Lots of jobs available. Also well-researched information on over 3,000 companies. The site had 35,000 jobs listed when I reviewed it. Lots of industry job boards.

Fast and accurate job search engine. No need to register to use services. This site has some amazing, well-written articles about all kinds of topics relating to careers and job searches.

OTHER JOB SEARCH SITES:

- **www.4work.com**: The site seems to have an emphasis on entry-level or internship positions. The job listings repeated the same postings 4 or 5 in a row. As a sample of search results, there were 48 marketing positions in Boston (including duplicates, so probably only 14 actual). As for the job search engine, you can only select 1 state or city at a time so if you are looking in multiple locations you are out of luck.

  We received slow and mixed up "accounting" searches; the results gave account managers positions, not necessarily accounting positions. There were also missing pages. Overall, not the best experience.

- **www.6figurejobs.com**: Good niche site for business executives looking for $100,000+ compensation (not a bad gig!). You can select more than one job interest field and location with the search engine. It has an easy-to-understand listing of jobs, location and date posted. Worth checking out for senior executives.

- **http://about.com/careers**: This site has many separate links for career planning and job searching. Click on one of the links and get search information along with informative articles. This isn't a site where you search for jobs, rather a portal to the many sites you can visit to actually search for specific positions.

- **www.actionjobs.com**: "The place to go when your job sucks." $39.95 to join what is called the #1 site for adventure employment service. Some links are for fishing jobs in Alaska, outdoor jobs and action-packed jobs. They'll extend your membership for 6 months free if you don't get a job. Overall, lots of content, but you'll need to click a few times to find a site to search for a position (and you'll be bombarded with pop ups each time you click!).

- **www.Aftercollege.com**: (formerly called **www. thejobresource.com)** You have to register to search for jobs. Mostly for seniors in college and recent graduates. Has an alumni network, which is a good concept, just not sure how active it is. University of Rhode Island search yielded 1 alumnus.

- **www.Americanjobs.com**: You can select only 1 career interest field and state. Our search resulted in no marketing jobs in DC, one in Boston, and two for New York. Another search yielded only 5 accounting positions in NY and 1 in PA. Only 2 computer programmer jobs in PA, no computer e-commerce positions.

  Results also had a lot of duplicate positions. Many of the job postings were a bit old showing post dates from 3-5 months ago. Overall, not the best experience.

- **www.Analyzemycareer.com**: Not a job search site, but overall good place to research what you want to do and what type of jobs are best for you. There are many profiles and tests you can take in order to find that perfect job, but keep in mind they charge a fee.

- **www.aarp.org/moneyguide**: This is a good resource for 50+ year-olds looking for information and resources regarding careers and money. There is no job search aspect to this site, though.

- **www.Bestjobsusa.com**: I'd recommend signing up for the jobsifter feature to get an automatic email sent to you when available positions matching your qualifications are posted. It's easy and you don't have to give up a lot of time and personal information to sign up. They just ask for your name and email address along with what state and career field you're interested in.

The search engine is simple and so are the results, maybe slightly oversimplified. You get more information when you click for details. We found lots of old jobs. When reviewing, we clicked on five separate positions and each was posted almost a year ago. We could only find a few new ones that were posted in the past month. Only 6 of 96 total postings were posted in past month. Stick with the job alert email signup for the newest postings.

- **www.bigjobs.net:** This is a small portal site with links to three job search sites: Flipdog, Work at home site and College recruiter site.

- **www.brassring.com**: This easy-to-navigate site has a high quantity of job postings. Emphasis seems to skew a bit more on the high-tech side of things, but worthwhile for most job searchers. Check out their Brassring career events too.

- **www.careerexchange.com:** This has a clear and easy to search engine. Applying for jobs is a simple process since you do not need to become a member or give out lots of information. From our general searches, the job selection is limited, though.

- **www.career.com:** Site states it is the "world's first recruitment site." Overall this site had a limited amount of jobs. The search engine and listings were not as polished as other sites.

- **www.careers.org:** A very dense and content heavy site. Lots of information and links if you can navigate through it. Plus many regional links, if you are looking in a specific area. I even found some job search gems that I didn't know about before going to this site. They need to make it a bit easier to review and navigate, but overall it's full of good information. Great listing of over 300 major employer job telephone hotlines.

- **www.careerbabe.com:** The "Career babe" is your personal career advisor. You can send her a question and get it answered by the expert herself. More of a resource site, not necessarily a job search site. This site seems to be down as of the most recent reviews. We are unsure if it is temporary or permanent.

- **www.careerbuzz.com:** This site was better than we expected since we weren't too familiar with the URL. The design and general presentation are a bit funky, especially with the "chillin" section of horoscopes, trivia, etc. There were more than 200 marketing jobs when we did a sample search. The job listings were easy to understand, but the search function should allow you to narrow further your selection. Overall, worthwhile to check out.

- **www.careercity.com:** This site is extensive and easy to use. You can select multiple fields and job locations when you click on "advanced search." Additional results are pulled in from Hotjobs and other well-known sites. One odd thing we found was that they don't have job posted dates for many of the positions so you don't know when the job was posted. This adds a level of uncertainty to your efforts since you are unsure if the position is current or irrelevant.

- **www.careermosaic.com:** (same as **careerbuilder. com/headhunter.net**)

- **www.careerpath.com:** (same as **careerbuilder. com/headhunter.net**)

- **www.careershop.com:** This is one of the smaller job sites based on the amount of job listings we found. Only 60 engineering jobs throughout the entire U.S. There were less than 20 positions each for telemarketing, telecommunications, medical, retail and human resources. There were a lot of technical positions, so there seems to be a technical spin. CareerShop has an interesting web-based training partnership with MindLeaders worth checking out. Also, there is an online job fair section with over 50 cities and states listed.

- **www.careermag.com:** Site pulls job listings from **Wetfeet.com, Brassring.com,** and **Dice.com** to name a few. The search engine is limited in selection and our searches yielded only a moderate quantity of listings. The site's homepage is quite busy and a little overwhelming with its many links. They have numerous articles and advice columns that you can utilize for additional knowledge.

- **www.Careersite.com:** Good company profiles and also descriptions of skills needed for many positions, but not a site I would recommend as a priority. There are no drop down boxes for selecting what state or field you are interested in so you have to type out the information. The search was confusing and results gave me many jobs outside of the state I requested. The "should contain" vs. "must contain" vs. "must not contain" options for selection are confusing.

- **www.Cooljobs.com:** A good site for a targeted group of people looking for non-traditional jobs. This is definitely for the younger audience. Neat site, but not worth much of your time unless you are really interested in a non-traditional job, such as teaching tennis at Club Med or being a performer for Cirque du Soleil. Very simple, clutter-free site. Easy on the eyes. Cool.

- **www.coolworks.com:** Cool site as its name implies. Site states it has over 75,000 jobs in great places. You can search and link to jobs in specific locations and also choose jobs by categories such as national parks, jobs at water and ski resorts.

- **www.diversitylink.com:** Good initiative to bring female and minority professionals together with employers who have job opportunities. The site doesn't have the most robust search engine. You can only choose from categories and not geographic locations. At the time of our review, there were only 10 sales/marketing jobs and 4 health services positions available throughout the U.S.

- **www.directjobs.com:** Has a little over 8,000 total jobs posted. You have to register to apply for positions. There were only nine marketing jobs in an eight state search we conducted. Just 35 accounting jobs in the entire U.S. over the past month. Doesn't give posting dates, but you can select a time period when narrowing your search.

- **www.employersonline.com:** We found a limited selection of positions. Easy to submit your resume when applying for positions. A lot of positions had salary ranges shown up front which is nice and unfortunately a rarity on most job sites.

- **www.employmentwizard.com:** Overall ok site, it displays advertisements for different newspapers. Good connections with hometown newspapers and local businesses.

- **www.fedworld.gov:** Department of Commerce site that does many things, including posting federal jobs. Updated daily.

- **www.funjobs.com:** "Love your job. Love your life," as the homepage states. There are 379 total jobs listed on the site with the newest one being two weeks sold. A sample listing of positions include: Personal trainer, nanny and sales positions for 24-hour fitness gym which amounted to half of the jobs posted.

- **www.globalcareers.com:** Site says it is the premier Internet specialty recruitment service. It was under renovations when visited, so we weren't able to gather much information. Check it out when you read this and maybe it will be live.

- **www.gojobs.com:** This site is really for recruiters and not for jobhunters. There were only two marketing jobs, three healthcare jobs and a few more in sales and IT. Overall, the selection was limited.

- **www.guru.com:** You can create job alerts that will send an email to notify you when relevant positions are posted. The site had a good amount of positions available. The site stated over 50,000 in their marketplace and over 150,000 jobs online were being offered.

- **www.homeworkers.org**: The Independent Homeworkers Alliance (IHA) offers this members-only site. To gain access, you are required to join the organization for approximately $20/month. This site advertises itself as the world's largest freelance database of positions. One thing is for sure, they a lot of pop-up advertisements.

- **www.ivillage.com:** This site offers lots of articles and advice for women. The job search section is powered by **careerbuilder.com**. Click on the "work" tab to begin the search.

- **www.iccweb.com:** Site states that it is the oldest and first online career advice service. Site has many links to job sites and also lists businesses for sale. You have to register to use most services. Interesting industry reports detailing specifics of working in certain job fields. No registration is required to read those articles.

- **www.jobs.com:** Seems to really just emphasize the "blast-my-resume" service, which sends your resume to 1000s of recruiters. The cost is $49.

- **www.jobdirect.com:** Focuses completely on entry-level jobs. Now called True Careers. You have to answer many questions and fill out forms before you can search for jobs. Four long steps to register and then search. Site says it has over 30,000 positions for college and graduate students.

- **www.jobfactory.com:** Site states it has over 3.1 million job postings. Our sample search in DC for marketing positions search yielded only three jobs. "Construction" search in Texas yielded 40 positions. Not the greatest search options since you only have a field in which to type job title, city and state.

Results don't show posting dates or even how many positions the search yielded, so you don't know if there are 50 positions or 1,000. You receive much more information when you click on "details." There are links to other job search sites along with links to classified ads and recruiter postings. The site probably does have a lot of postings, it just needs to be a little more user-friendly.

- **www.jobfind.com:** Site specific to Massachusetts area. Skews towards healthcare and IT professionals from our review. The search is easy and the search results format is similar to the higher-quality job search sites.

- **www.jobfinders.com:** The first pay-per-click job site. Job search option was not up and running at the time we first reviewed this site. During our second visit, there was a message stating "Because **JobFinders.com** just opened, it will take a few weeks for jobs to fill up! Thanks for your patience. In the meantime, have you posted your resume?" Interesting concept, but don't have much to report at this time.

- **www.joboptions.com:** Average site with low to moderate amount of positions posted. Our search results yielded only 40 marketing jobs total in the U.S. and 30 were from the same 2 companies. Just 20 engineering positions throughout the U.S.

- **www.jobreports.net:** "Over 85% of all jobs are not published," this site claims. **Jobreports.net** helps you get into "the hidden market" as it calls it. Most of the 85% of jobs were filled by networking or through recruiters. You can get a sales/marketing report that lists the available positions and information for a fee. Similar to expensive magazine subscriptions, where you receive a report each month.

The company in charge of this site is *Faith, Winter and Grace Inc.* They are a full-service career agency for one-on-one assistance, resume review or job search assistance.

- **www.jobsonline.com:** You can search for jobs and get a summary of positions available, but you have to register to get detailed information on the jobs including where and how to apply. We found 132 marketing jobs throughout the U.S. in the past 30 days, 500 in accounting and 17 in engineering. You need to register to utilize any of the services, including resources and articles. Overall, good site despite the need to register.

- **www.jobweb.org:** From the National Association of Colleges and Employers, this site concentrates on the younger job applicant market, i.e., college and recent graduates. Doesn't list actual positions, but gives many links and articles relating to student job searches.

- **www.kellyservices.com:** This international site states they have found 158,000 jobs for people this year. You can set up a search agent and store your resume. Moderate size list of temporary and full-time jobs available.

- **www.manpower.com:** This Fortune 500 staffing services company has a site that breaks out your search: Manpower and manpower professional depending on what type of position you are looking for. Has free skills assessment offer on site. Didn't have much luck finding jobs on this site. Yielded either zero positions, or only 1 or 2 positions per state, for certain jobs.

- **www.imdiversity.com:** "**IMDiversity.com** was conceived by *The Black Collegian* Magazine, which has provided African-American college students with valuable information on career and job opportunities since 1970." Good niche site that has virtual communities tailored to specific ethnic groups. Daily news, special reports and lots of informative resources. Overall quantity of job postings seems to be pretty good compared to other niche sites.

- **www.nationjob.com:** This has the most detailed search for geographic location I've seen. Results aren't easily readable. You don't know upfront when they were posted or what the company is. Once you click on positions, the detail page is well set up, though you still do not know the posting date so the job could already be filled or obsolete. Especially good for techie folks.

- **www.net-temps.com:** Mostly temporary jobs (hence the site name) with some full-time jobs. Job detail states length of assignment. If you don't click the button to have jobs sorted by posting date, you get an odd prioritization with dates all over the place. We did a keyword search of "marketing," but many of the positions listed did not have anything to do with marketing, nor did they have the keyword "marketing" in the title or description.

- **www.opportunitynocs.org:** Concentrates on jobs with non-profits. Only 580 jobs listed nationwide when it was reviewed. One job in Florida and Virginia. There were 105 jobs in Pennsylvania and just 7 jobs in Washington D.C.

- **www.preferredjobs.com:** Overall pretty good site with a significant amount of opportunities in various fields from accounting to sales. The site has lots of ways to search for positions. There are no drop down boxes for state or city so you're not sure if the computer understands what you are typing. Pretty clear job descriptions.

- **www.recruiterresources.com:** One stop resource for recruiters and HR Managers. Links to job search sites, resume databases and search engines. This site has a lot of what appears to be good links to other sites, but we found many of the links were bad and received errors when clicked.

- **www.recruitersonline.com:** This site offers an easy way to reach recruiters and to search for employment professionals worldwide. Even if you don't see listings that interest you, you can find out recruiter's names and email addresses to send them your resume for future reference.

- **www.resweb.com**: Have to register to search for jobs. Tried to register 3 times, but got an error each time. You can also post a resume for free, if you dare. Has a resume locator service for which it charges. Good option for busy recruiters.

- **www.saludos.com:** Site dedicated to serving the Hispanic market. Great to see these types of niche job sites. Has some good resources, much from its magazine, "Saludos Hispanos Magazine." As for job postings, it runs a little low. We found no jobs in marketing in DC and PA, 1 job in MA. 0 positions in customer service for California.

- **www.tjobs.com:** This is a niche site for telecommuters. Check it out if that's what you are interested in doing.

- **www.upseek.com:** This is a cool site with good technology. Neat way to sort results by websites and company sites.

- **www.wetfeet.com:** Good resource for career advice and company research. Limited job postings from our review. Some good discussion boards and self-assessment tests.

Major portal job sites:

- **Careers.yahoo.com**: We received good results from this free search site. You can sort results by company, date and salary, which is always nice. Good open database for posting on Yahoo Classifieds. Powered by **Careerbuilder.com**.

- America Online career center: keyword "career center." Powered by **Monster.com**. Same features as **Monster.com**.

State Employment Websites

Each state has its own website where you can search for positions working for the state government and in the private sector. Here is a listing for each state's job site:

Alabama: www.dir.state.al.us/es/default.htm	Alaska: www.jobs.state.ak.us
Arizona: www.ajb.org/az	Arkansas: www.ajb.org/ar
California: www.edd.cahwnet.gov/findjob.htm	Colorado: www.ajb.org/co
Connecticut: www.ctdol.state.ct.us	Delaware: www.vcnet.net/dafault.asp
DC: www.does.ci.washington.dc.us/main.shtm	Florida: www2.myflorida.com/default.html
Georgia: www.dol.state.ga.us	Hawaii: www.ajb.org/hi
Idaho: www.labor.state.id.us	Illinois: www.ajb.org/il
Indiana: www.ajb.org/in	Iowa: www.state.ia.us/jobs
Kansas: www.kansasjobs.org	Kentucky: www.desky.org/jobsrch/jobsrch.htm
Louisiana: www.ajb.org/la	Maine: www.mainecareercenter.com
Maryland: www.ajb.org/md	Massachusetts: www.ajb.org/ma
Michigan: www.michigan.gov/mdcd	Minnesota: www.des.state.mn.us
Mississippi: www.ajb.org/ms	Missouri: www.works.state.mo.us/mw2a.htm
Montana: jsd.dli.state.mt.us	Nebraska: www.ajb.org/ne
Nevada: www.detr.state.nv.us	New Hampshire: www.nhworks.state.nh.us
New Jersey: www.ajb.org/nj	New Mexico: www.ajb.org/nm
New York: www.labor.state.ny.us	North Carolina: www.esc.state.nc.us
North Dakota: www.state.nd.us/jsnd	Ohio: www.stateofohiojobs.com
Oklahoma: www.oesc.state.ok.us/okjobnet	Oregon: www.emp.state.or.us
Pennsylvania: www.ajb.org/pa	Rhode Island: www.det.state.ri.us
South Carolina: www.sces.org	South Dakota: www.state.sd.us/dol/dol.htm
Tennessee: www.state.tn.us/labor-wfd	Texas: www.twc.state.tx.us/twc.html
Utah: www.dws.state.ut.us	Vermont: www.det.state.vt.us
Virginia: www.vec.state.va.us	Washington: www.wa.gov/esd/employment.html
West Virginia: www.ajb.org/wv	Wisconsin: www.dwd.state.wi.us/jobnet/mapwi.htm
Wyoming: onestop.state.wy.us/appview/wjn_home.asp	

Specialized job search sites

Not getting the results you'd like in the major job sites? Are you looking for a targeted job or a non-traditional position? Here is a listing of some niche sites that may guide you in the right direction:

Accounting/Finance:
www.accountemps.com

www.accountingjobs.com
www.finance-jobs.net

Advertising/Media:
www.allmediastaffing.com
www.aquent.com

Arts/Entertainment:
www.4entertainmentjobs.com
www.arthire.com
www.showbizjobs.com

Computers/IT:
www.computerworld.com
www.dice.com
www.justtechjobs.com: Connected to **www.justwebjobs.com**.

Education:
www.academploy.com
www.adjunctnation.com
www.jobsineducation.com

Engineering:
www.contractengineering.com
www.engineeringjobs.com

Medical/Health:
www.medsearch.com: Part of **Monster.com**.
www.4nursingjobs.com
www.hirehealth.com
www.healthjobsusa.com

Overseas:
www.escapeartist.com
www.overseasjobs.com (this site is part of **aboutjobs.com** which also includes: **internjobs.com, summerjobs.com** and **resortjobs.com**)

Sales/Marketing:
www.jobs4sales.com
www.marketingjobs.com
www.marketingpower.com(ama)

Temps/Freelance:
www.acountemps.com
www.elance.com
www.freelanceonline.com
www.guru.com

This is just a summary listing of a few specialized job search sites. I urge you to utilize one of the better search engines like **Google.com** to find other sites that may tie in directly to your job niche.

Top 10 online job search mistakes

1. Sending resume only as an attachment.

2. Not following-up after sending information to a potential employer.

3. Not testing job search engines with various keywords to find the most effective method that yields the jobs you are targeting.

4. Posting your resume on sites without regard to privacy, especially if you are currently employed.

5. Not spending the appropriate amount of time preparing your resume and cover letter to email. Just because you can now do certain aspects of job searching much faster than in the past, it doesn't mean you should skimp on proofreading and targeting. It's very easy to send out 5 resumes in 15 minutes, but don't do it.

6. Not checking your email daily and/or returning phone calls in order to respond quickly to inquiries.

7. Not using the many search agents offered on job sites that send you email updates about specific jobs which may interest you. You shouldn't rely solely on this option, but it is a good complement to your regular search and it saves time.

8. Not asking for the interviewer's business card so you can send a thank you email within 24 hours of your interview.

9. Not printing out job descriptions that you replied to and organizing the Who, What, Where of communications between you and potential employers.

10. Getting frustrated and down on yourself when the going gets tough.

> **TIP: Click on the option "all opportunities in this company" on job search sites such as monster.com. This gives you a better idea of what positions a company has open.**

Phone calls and job searching

If your job search includes calling people and talking on the phone, make sure your goal of the conversation is to move to the next step of scheduling a meeting in person.

Make sure you get the names of every person you speak with on the phone or through email. You can always reference that person and network yourself to get to the key hiring people for example, "Mr. Smith suggested I speak to you to set up an interview."

You need to be a salesperson. Sell yourself. Don't accept the first negative response as a rejection, continue to ask questions. If the particular person does not have an opening, ask if any other departments in the company have something that might be a good fit. Does the person

know of other companies or contacts he may be able to give you to follow-up?

TIP: Look through papers and trade magazines in the career news or promo-
tions sections for good job-hunting contacts. You can see who has recently
gotten promoted at different companies.

It's always a great idea to send an email to someone who you believe
would be a potential hiring contact in order to congratulate the person
on his or her promotion. Send a simple email stating that you read
about his or her promotion in (title) magazine and you wanted to congratulate them and also submit your resume in case they have a need
for a hard working employee.

CHAPTER 3—SUMMARY

- Stay organized when searching for a job. Print or cut out job postings and place in a folder. If you have not heard from the employer in three to four weeks, follow-up with a short email that has your resume pasted at the end of the message. If you hear back from an employer that has decided not to move forward with your candidacy, place the job postings in another folder to store for future reference.

- Top recommended general job sites: **Monster.com**, **Hotjobs.com**, America's job bank, **Careerbuilder.com** and **Vault.com** to name a few.

- There are general job search sites and then there are also niche job sites for specific careers. There are also job sites for each state.

- Some of the top online job search mistakes include: Sending a resume only as an attachment, not following-up after sending information, posting your resume without regard to privacy and not spending the appropriate amount of time targeting your resume and cover letter to the specific position.

4

Interview preparation and follow-up

You've written down what type of job you want. You've created an excellent resume and effective cover letter. You've searched through the miles of websites and classified ads, all to come to this point. You have an interview! Congratulate yourself and get ready for the next stage: Interviewing.

Don't be afraid--it won't be that bad. If you're new to this whole job interview thing, don't worry, I've been through it and will guide you through each stage. If you are more experienced, there's always room for improvement.

> *"Eighty percent of success is showing up."*
> *Woody Allen*

There are five core questions an interviewer is attempting to answer during the interview phase. Martin Yate discusses these five key areas in his book *Knock 'em Dead 2002*. "During an interview, employers ask you dozens of searching questions--questions that test your confidence, poise, and desirable personality traits...They are all designed so that the interviewer can make decisions on some critical areas:"

- Can you do the job?

- Will you complement or disrupt the department?

- Are you willing to take the extra step?

- Are you manageable?

- Is the money right?

As we go through this chapter and during your interviews, think about these questions and do your best to make sure the answer to each of the questions is a positive one.

A. Pre-interview stage

Research before heading to your interview

As you're preparing for your interview, make sure you find out additional information on the company. Here are a few methods of doing this:

- Go directly to the company's website. Type in the exact company name and add a ".com" (or a ".org" if it's non-profit) and you'll probably find it. If not, head to a search engine like **www. google.com** and type in the company name, most likely you will be able to locate it there.

- There are a few websites out there that concentrate on business and corporate research: **www.companiesonline.com**, **www.hoovers.com**, **www.comfind.com** or **www.bizweb.com**.

Few tidbits for you to keep in mind when you get that call from a potential employer to set up the interview:

1. Thank the person on the other end of the line for selecting you to come in for an interview. Be enthusiastic. Even if you don't recall exactly what was entailed in the position, smile and be excited. You can always find out the details later.

2. Make sure you clearly understand the name of the company and the title of the position so you can check back in your "follow-up" folder to review the exact job description.

3. Ask the person what their full name and phone number is in case you need to change plans or have a follow-up question. An email address wouldn't hurt either.

4. Ask what the appropriate dress is for the interview. Some companies may want the traditional suit and tie or dress, while others prefer casual pant and shirt/blouse combination. If you are not clear, it is always best to err on the more conservative side and wear at least a shirt/tie or dress, if not a business suit.

5. Ask who you will be interviewing with and how many interviews are scheduled. It is always good to know in advance if you are having one interview with an HR representative or if you have a marathon interview schedule where eight separate interviews are set up for you!

6. It has been said that the last applicant who interviews for the position has a better chance of being hired. You stand out more in the people's mind. Try to set up the interview to be the last or one of the last people. I wouldn't recommend asking outright if you could be the last applicant, rather casually ask the person making the appointment what is the overall interview schedule timeframe.

7. Lastly, it is always good to follow-up a phone call with an email stating that you are looking forward to meeting him or her along with the other representatives and confirm the date and time.

Behavioral interviewing

While the title sounds a little scary, it's nothing to be afraid of, just be prepared. The whole interview process is risky for both the job applicant and also for the company hiring. Decisions, about whom is best

)sition and which company to choose, need to be made after only a few short discussions.

In order to take advantage of the limited amount of time spent with applicants, many employers have begun to ask their questions in a particular format. Hence the birth of behavioral interviewing.

The general idea behind behavioral interviewing is that a person's past job performance is the best predictor of his or her future behavior at work. If a company is looking for "critical thinkers" or "self starters," they want to hear about specific situations in the recent past where you displayed your ability to think critically or showed initiative.

> *"You can tell whether a man is clever by his answers. You can tell whether a man is wise by his questions."*
> *Mahfouz Naguib*

Employers using behavioral interviewing tend to ask very specific questions about recent professional experience and follow-up by asking for details. You will notice the interviewer asks for a significant amount of detail and follows up with probing questions to get at exactly what you said, what you did, etc. Some sample questions an interviewer might ask are:

- Tell me about a time you faced a challenge at work. What did you do?

- Describe a recent experience at work when you disagreed with your supervisor. What did you do?

- Give me an example of a recent project you worked on that required significant attention to detail. What was it? What did you do?

As you can see from the above sample questions, the interviewer concentrates on recent examples and asks open-ended questions with follow-up details.

What can I do to excel in a behavioral interview?

- Prior to the interview, prepare by identifying what critical behaviors your potential employer may believe are important. Re-read the job posting for clues.

- Brainstorm recent events in your career where you demonstrated these behaviors. Also, identify other critical career moments that show other traits you possess (i.e. the time you saved the company thousands of dollars with an idea).

- Be honest and avoid embellishing your stories. Since the interviewer will be probing for more detail, resist making up other aspects to round out the experience. Behavioral interviewers are trained to know when an applicant is lying.

- During the interview, listen carefully for what the interviewer is asking. If they ask for detail, make sure you provide him or her with the level of detail they want. If you are unsure, simply ask them if your response adequately answered their question. Don't be afraid to ask questions when you are unclear.

> **TIP: Bring along breath mints or mouthwash to freshen your breath a few minutes before going into a company. Make sure you dispose of anything before you begin the interview. Don't have something in your mouth while you are interviewing.**

Informational interviews

Sometimes a good strategy is to work toward an informational interview. If you're having a difficult time getting an interview with that company you really want to work for, try this out. Here are a few ways you can work on scheduling an informational interview:

- Review the company website and click on any listings showing management or employment information. If it's a small company, most of the staff might be listed right there on the site. If it is a larger firm, you might only be able to get a phone number for Human Resources.

Email or call the person in the department that fits your experience. Discuss briefly that you are extremely interested in Company X and would like the opportunity to sit down briefly with Ms. Z to ask a few questions about the industry and how she attained that position. Flattery is always good.

• Networking: As we discussed in Chapter 2, you can make great strides in landing an interview or job by networking. Good places to network are at professional association events, church, volunteer organizations, along with attending sports events or even cocktail hours (just watch your intake!).

B. During the Interview Stage

When you arrive at the company for your interview, after you introduce yourself to person at front desk, ask for the directions to the bathroom. This will give you a chance to, hopefully be by yourself, look in the mirror to make sure everything is okay and take time to breath and relax after your car ride. It also lets your mind focus on the upcoming discussion.

> TIP: Make sure you make copies of your resume on good quality paper and bring them to the interview. You also need a pen and a pad of paper to take notes.

When it comes to the actual interview, you need to make a positive impression immediately. Christopher Jones, author of *Interviewing With Body Language*, asks:

"How long do you have to prove yourself in an interview? Half an hour? Fifteen minutes? University of Toledo researchers found that job seekers have under 30 seconds to make their mark on interviewers. Since first impressions are sometimes made before job seekers even open their mouths, nonverbal communication—or, body language—is an essential part of any interview."

"In the book of life, the answers aren't in the back."
Charlie Brown

I recently spoke with one of my employer contacts who was previously a human resources recruiter for one of the big five consulting firms. He shared with me some of his biggest turnoffs when it comes to resumes and interviews:

1. Applicants who ask canned questions and really don't show interest in the answer.

2. Flashy resumes with too many distracting "bells and whistles."

3. Arrogance during the interview.

4. Spelling mistakes.

5. Lack of organization in resumes.

6. Resumes that are too sterile.

He goes on to say, "I've always encouraged applicants to include a few interests, skills or activities that would help me or the recruiter understand what that person is all about. Just be concise."

> **TIP: Interviewers hire people they like and are comfortable with. Try to find a common bond with people at each company.**

What to do during the interview

Relax, smile and keep eye contact with the interviewer. This doesn't mean you should stare at the person and never look away (that would be a little freaky for the person on the other side of the desk!). A confident interviewee keeps eye contact when listening and speaking while taking a few, needed breaks by looking down to take notes for example.

Take a few quick notes during the interview. Write the person's name on top of the sheet and then a few bullet points. Utilize these notes when you are writing your follow-up thank you email/letter. Bringing up specific conversation topics you had or reiterating certain comments the interviewer made, gives you extra points in the eyes of the employer and also shows that you are a good listener.

Interviewing is a two-way relationship. They want an employee and you want an employer. Ask questions to make sure they are the right company for you. Don't simply make up 1 or 2 questions to ask just because you think it's the right thing to do. Ask questions that mean something to you.

You don't want to accept a job only to find out you're dealing with the same problems as your last job. Learn from your experiences and mistakes to ensure the next position is better. Each new job is another stepping-stone in your life and career.

As Ron Gregory, VP and Senior Consultant at Dunhill Professional Search, states: "Ask for the job!" When your interview is winding down, express enthusiasm for the position. Adding that last positive statement may give you a small added boost from 98% to 100% approval. Statements like "I love your company and have been a loyal customer for years" or "This position is exactly what I am looking for," or "I can definitely see myself as a Detail Inc team member" can give you the boost you need.

At the end of an interview, ask for their business card and also what the next steps are in the interviewing process, including timeframe for making a hiring decision.

C. Post-Interview Stage

You made it through the interview. Congratulations, you've taken another successful step in getting your new job. It is extremely important to follow-up immediately after your interview.

Sending a thank you follow-up has these positive outcomes:

• Your interviewer will be reminded of who you are.

• You have a chance to reiterate your desire for the position and highlight your qualifications.

• The majority of people do not send thank you follow-ups, so you will be ahead of the applicants when it comes down to deciding.

In the current work environment, either traditional printed and mailed thank you letters or emails are appropriate.

Here are a few examples of thank you letters or emails.

Thank you letter/email #1

February 19, 200X

Dear Mr. Claire:

(A)

Thank you for taking time out of your busy schedule to meet with me yesterday afternoon. I enjoyed our conversation and also the chance to learn more about GSS Inc.

(B)

As we discussed in the interview, the key to success in this position is the ability to manage multiple projects at once. My previous experience at XYZ Company helped me acquire the skill of juggling many tasks and I believe this is one of the biggest assets I have to offer.

(C)

Again, thank you for the chance to discuss the Manager position and I look forward to speaking with you soon.

Sincerely,

Thomas J. Paige

Author's Comments:

As you can see, the thank you follow-up is short and to the point. In the first section (A), your objective is to thank them and also remind them of who you are by stating a specific time period when you met. The second section (B) is your opportunity to reiterate one of the key points that was specific to your one-on-one conversation. Incorporate one of the key comments from your notes you took during the interview. In the last section (C), you simply close the letter and again remind the person of the position applied for and leave the door open for either party to follow-up.

Thank you letter/email #2

April 1, 200X

Dear Ms. Dybul:

I appreciated the chance to meet with you face to face today to discuss further the position of Manufacturing Engineer. The meeting confirmed my initial positive beliefs about PLF Enterprises and clarified your objectives for this important position.

I would like to reiterate my strong desire to work for PLF Enterprises as it is a place I can see myself growing and contributing to the company's success for many years. You have an excellent team and I would like to be a part of its future.

Again, thank you for the chance to discuss the position and I look forward to speaking with you soon.

Sincerely,

Marc Kandy

Author's Comments:

Complimenting always works. ☺

References—Available upon request

"References Available upon Request" has long been an obligatory statement made at the end of resumes, but over the past few years the statement has disappeared from many resumes. Quite honestly, the statement is not particularly necessary in today's environment. It's assumed that you have, or will have, references available when you are asked to furnish them to an employer.

You should have references (preferably three) available before an employer requests them from you. When an employer does actually ask you for your references, make sure they are typed in a clear and concise fashion. The information you need to supply for references includes:

- The reference's full name

- Phone number and email

- What your relationship is with this person.

In addition, call each of your references first and get their permission to be one of your references. You don't want them to be surprised when, out of the blue, a potential employer calls them for information on your track record. If they agree, thank them and inform them that they may be getting a phone call soon. Let your references know:

- What is the position title

- What is the name of the company

- What are some of the details and qualifications the company is looking for in this position.

You've done a great job so far and have worked very hard in order to get to this stage. Keep the positive momentum going with a well-prepared group of references.

Good things come to those who wait. Keep a positive attitude.

The job market can be tough at times and some people may get frustrated because they have not received as many responses as expected. From my experience, here is what tends to happen:

- Probably 20% of the positions are never filled due to various internal and external reasons. Jobs are put on hold. Companies decide they don't have money in the budget, etc.

- Approximately 25% are filled internally, but had to be advertised to the public due to corporate policies.

With these assumptions, that leaves a job applicant with a little more than 50% of an opportunity to get a call for an interview. Don't get angry if you have been rejected for interviews or don't get many call-backs.

> *"Most people give up just when they're about to achieve success. They quit on the one yard line. They give up at the last minute of the game one foot from a winning touchdown."*
> **H. Ross Perot**

Here are a few positive steps you can take when you find yourself in this position:

- Edit and improve resumes and cover letters with newly acquired knowledge from speaking with people.

- Continue searching through all of the channels listed in Chapter 1.

- Try new things, such as attending job fairs or doing temporary work.

- Keep in mind that the next resume you send could be the one that gets you a job.

Janet Garber, in her book *I Need a Job, Now What?* discusses "Beating the Rejection Blues" by remembering the following:

1. In most instances the reason you do not get any given job has nothing to do with you personally….just get on to the next possibility.

2. Understand that anyone you met while job hunting can become a valuable contact later in your career. So consider the hunt part of networking and try to enjoy getting to know people you meet during your job search.

3. Remember, there's a distinct probability that all this hard work will eventually land you in a better job than you've ever had before.

CHAPTER 4—SUMMARY

- Pre-Interview: Do research on the company before going to your interview. **www.companiesonline.com** and **www.hoovers.com** are good sites for this. Prepare a list of questions for the employer and review some of the interview questions in the chapter. Make copies of your resume and bring along a notepad and pen.

- During the Interview: You have less than 30 seconds to make a good impression. Be confident and relaxed. Have a firm and confident handshake. Try to build a rapport by finding similar interests between you and the interviewer. Ask for the job at the end. There are many effective ways of showing the employer your interest.

- Post-Interview: Send thank you follow-up with 24 hours. Keep it short.

- Have at least three professional references typed up and ready to distribute.

- Keep a positive attitude when going through difficult job search times. Edit resumes and cover letters with recent feedback. Continue to move forward and your hard work will be rewarded.

5

Negotiation and job offer acceptance

"Let us not negotiate out of fear, but let us never fear to negotiate."
President JOHN F. KENNEDY

We've been through the challenging times of deciding what your next job should look like. We've created perfect resumes and cover letters. We continued onto the nerve-racking interview phase and now you can see the peak of the "job search mountain." You've gotten a job offer. A chance to begin anew and show the company what you can do.

Here's our #1 rule:

• Never accept the first offer an employer gives you for a job. Even if you're extremely interested in the position and the salary and/or benefits are more than you expected, simply say "thank you for the offer" and let them know you need to think about it and will get back to them in the next couple days. There are, of course, exceptions, but follow this rule the majority of the time.

If you are a real expert in the game of negotiation, you can always put your high school acting training to good use and act a bit shocked or in slight disbelief when you hear the offer. Something to the nature of "Oh. I was thinking it would have been higher" or possibly just a simple, targeted "hmmm" will do the job.

An alternative is asking if there is room for negotiation. This communicates to the employer that you may be looking for a higher salary and prepares them for your follow-up phone call when you do, indeed, ask for that increase.

When it comes to requesting a better offer, you can always err on the higher side. If you would accept a $1,000 higher salary, then ask for $1,500. You'll be amazed what you get when you ask for it. This doesn't mean you should ask for $5,000 more when you really only need $1,000. Keep it real and consistent with what comparable positions are paid.

Show me the money—How to increase your salary by $2,000 in 5 minutes or less

There's no better chance to negotiate a higher salary than before you accept the position. After you accept the position, 95% of the time you are stuck at that salary level for at least another year. Employers spend a lot of time and money trying to find the right candidate, so when they offer you a position, you have a lot of power for negotiation. They want you. Out of all the candidates, they chose you. Remember this when you're negotiating.

Too many people are afraid to discuss an increase or may feel they are not worth it. You are worth it. Even if it's only $500 more per year, it's worth the extra phone call. If you saw $500 on the street, wouldn't you pick it up? Sure you would. Well, with one simple phone call and a 2-minute conversation (actually people have told me they've actually left a voice message asking for more money), you can potentially increase your salary.

"If you want a better deal, ask for it…calmly and confidently."
Brian Tracy

When negotiating and finalizing the offer, get everything in writing. There have been times in my life when this came in handy. I negotiated a six-month salary review before accepting a previous position and because of communication troubles within the HR department, I ended up having to show management the offer letter in order to have the company address the situation.

Benefits—The hidden gem of job offers

On top of salary, there are, of course, many other aspects of the offer such as healthcare benefits, vacation time, bonuses, etc. Benefits can account for 25-50% of your salary depending on the company, so there is a huge opportunity for you in negotiating.

Here are a few benefits I've seen negotiated in job offers:

- An additional week of vacation time (you can never have too much!)

- Health benefits that begin immediately, rather than waiting 3-4 months to be eligible

- An increase in the annual bonus from 10 to 15% or attaining an agreement of a bonus when there was none previously

- Being able to contribute to 401K plan immediately, rather than waiting the 1 year time period traditionally required for new employees

- Relocation expenses for moving, along with reimbursement for paying off remaining money owed on a rental lease

- Use of a company car

- Additional stock options

- Position title change from Manager to Senior Manager or Manager to Director (whoever says titles don't matter, never went on interviews)

- An additional signing bonus. (Often companies won't be able to increase your salary however, with a signing bonus, your base salary can remain within the range and you could get the extra cash you were looking for to get started)

- A three or six month salary review. This shorter time period for an evaluation gives the company a chance to ensure that your skills are worth what you say they are and, more importantly, gives you a chance to prove your value

I give you these examples just to get your creative juices flowing when it comes time to negotiate. You certainly shouldn't ask for all of these, but each job offer will lend itself to a few of these.

Handle with care

My recommendation is to handle each negotiation point separately. Here's an example: If you want $2,000 more on your salary and also more vacation time, first concentrate on the most important. In this case, let's say it's the $2,000 increase. Go to sites like **www.salary.com** to find out the salary range for a comparable position. Assuming the information works to your advantage, print out the pages and utilize them in your negotiation.

"Never accept the first offer, no matter how good it sounds. Never reject an offer out of hand, no matter how unacceptable it sounds at first."
Brian Tracy

Rather than telling the employer you want $2,000 more because you think you're worth it, show them. "Mr. Wyatt, I want to thank you again for the offer and let you know I'm extremely interested in the position. You had said you might be open to a discussion on salary and I would like to address it now if you are willing..."

After he says "Yes," begin with "I've been doing some research and also speaking with others in the industry and someone with 5+ years experience and supervisory responsibility has a salary range of $X to $Y. As you can see the offer falls just short of $X and I was wondering if you would be able to offer $Z?" In this example, you did your research and gave him specifics on why you deserve more money.

After you have successfully negotiated the salary increase, it is now time to discuss your vacation time. It is preferred that this discussion happen separately and not during the same conversation regarding salary.

There aren't many specifics you can point to regarding vacation so this is more of a crapshoot. If you had more vacation time in your past position, it doesn't hurt to state, "In my previous position, I had 12 days of paid vacation per year. I found this benefit to be extremely important to me and it is one of the reasons why I stayed with the company for the past five years. Are we able to slightly increase the time by a few days?"

In closing, you don't want to come across as being too demanding and unreasonable. You are in a good position to negotiate a better deal, but it has to be fair. Keep this in mind when dealing with the prospective employer.

CHAPTER 5—SUMMARY

- Never accept the first offer an employer gives you for a job. Ask if there is room for negotiation.

- You'll be amazed at what additional benefits you can receive just by asking.

- There's no better time to increase your salary then right at the point where you are offered a job. Take advantage of this time period. They chose you over all the applicants. It's tough to find good employees and they believe they found one in you. The ball is in your court.

- Handle each negotiation point separately. You don't want to be seen as unreasonable by asking for too much all at once.

6

And beyond...

Build a future of success

Well, you did it! You found your perfect job. Congratulations. You should be proud of what you have accomplished. Make sure you reward yourself with that day spa visit you've been wanting or those tickets to your favorite sporting event. Whatever it is, take time to enjoy yourself.

> *"By working faithfully eight hours a day you may eventually get to be boss and work twelve hours a day."*
> *Robert Frost*

After the fun wears down, it's time to start your job. This should bring a smile to your face and not a frown as it may have previously. In order to make your present job the best it can be and also to prepare yourself for your next career move, let's discuss a few final points.

Prepare for your annual review every day

In order for you to get those big raises you will want in the next year or so, you need to create an *accomplishment folder*. Keep an actual folder with hard copies of emails, memos, reports or anything that shows concrete evidence of your accomplishments throughout the year. You can also keep an email folder where you can save positive emails you receive from associates and your supervisors.

If you get a complimentary email from someone, print it off and stick it in the folder or save it in your accomplishment email folder. If you created a report and presented it to management, place it in the folder or at least write yourself a note and put it in the folder stating the date and what you achieved. You should be able to note something worthwhile each week, or at least a couple times a month.

When it comes time for reviews, yours will be a snap. You've been writing it all year long. By keeping good notes on your accomplishments, you not only help yourself, but also your boss. Your boss can have many people reporting to him or her and may not remember all of the good things that you accomplished.

He will appreciate a very detailed accomplishment review sheet because it will make his job easier. I've had bosses who take my accomplishment sheet verbatim and utilize that as the majority of their written review. Talk about putting words in your boss' mouth!

Earn and learn: How to get a college or graduate degree for FREE

Many employers offer tuition reimbursement for employees. If you are lucky enough to have this benefit, take advantage of it. This is your chance to get FREE education and FREE knowledge. Even if it's only two classes per year, you now have additional skills and knowledge that you can highlight on your resume.

Remember in Chapter 1 when you were looking for a job and got frustrated because you didn't have the skills required in some of the job postings? Now is your chance to change and improve yourself.

Some of my previous employers have paid for my Master's degree courses and also Internet-related classes. I've attended leadership seminars and industry conferences, all paid for by the company. The employers are happy because they now have a better, more knowledgeable employee and you are happy because in addition to learning something new, you are also more marketable.

Keep setting goals

If you had a hard time networking during your job search, now is the time to start building those important relationships. Anytime someone leaves your company for another job or endeavor, make sure you ask for their home address, email or phone number. If you enjoyed working with them and vice versa, you now have a great start to your job network. Remember from Chapter 1, the majority of jobs are still filled through networking.

Make it a goal to build that contact list up to 5 or 10 contacts in the first year. Go back to old jobs and find out past associate's information and once you have it, send an email to let them know where you are now working. Ask for an update on their lives and how they are doing. Networking is a two-way street. You help them and they will help you; it's the way the world works.

Make a goal to communicate with your growing list of contacts at least once every 3 to 4 months. Even just a short email saying hello, summarizing the past few months at your job and then asking them about their life. You will be happy you kept in touch once that next job search comes around.

In closing

Well my friends, we near the end of this journey. I hope you have achieved everything you wanted to achieve. It is important to enjoy the work you do. Finding the perfect job will make your workday much more pleasurable and also make your life outside of work a better one.

Use this book as a motivational tool to push yourself to continue when, at times, you want to give up. Review this book when you aren't sure how to answer a question an employer asks. Lastly, take advantage of the resources detailed in these many pages.

CHAPTER 6—SUMMARY

- Congratulations! You have found your perfect job. Build on this success throughout the next year and beyond. Keep a file of accomplishments so that you are ready for your next job review.

- Learn and earn: Take advantage of company benefits offering tuition reimbursement. You get a FREE education and also increase your value in the eyes of your current employer and future employers.

- Continue networking so the next time you are in need of assistance you have a solid list of contacts.

Bonus Section
The Trickiest Interview Questions
and their Answers

1. "Why do you want to work here?"

This is where your time spent researching the company, previous to applying or coming in for the interview pays off. If you know anything specific about the person you are interviewing with, feel free to compliment the interviewer on their previous successes. You can state that you have heard good things about that person through previous associates and you would be excited to have the opportunity to work and learn from him or her.

With regard to the company, reply by choosing one or two positive attributes such as the company's focus on customer service or their sustained growth rate over the past ten years. You can state that these are the areas you find extremely important and you were happy to see that Company X had those attributes. As always position your answers with the company's benefit in mind. While the interviewer is asking why you want to work for the company, dedicate a portion of your answer to why the company should want you also.

2. "Tell me about yourself?"

This is usually the first or second question you are asked during the interview. Mostly the employer wants to "break the ice" by easing you into the interview by having you talk about something easy, like yourself! Well, as with any interview, there are always additional objectives and some of these may include:

- See how you handle yourself. Are you confident and well-spoken? Do you look the interviewer in the eyes when you speak or are you looking down?

- To find out more about your personality along with likes and dislikes outside of the regular business environment.

Be careful with your response. There is no need to go into personal items such as your marriage, kids, religion or political affiliations.

Spend half your time discussing personal aspects that the employer may not know from your resume, such as your love of world travel or your creative drawing skills.

While it is good to discuss these personal aspects, it's even better if they can relate to the job somehow. Maybe the job requires creativity and you can emphasize your qualifications for this job by discussing your art studio you have at home. The remaining half of the time responding to this question can be spent on discussing you, as an employee. Let the employer know that you are passionate about your work and take great pride in the success you have attained for your past employers.

3. "What are you looking for in your next job?"

Again, be honest here. There's no reason to make things up just to make the employer happy. If the job is not what you're looking for, then you don't want it. If you applied for the job and accepted the chance to meet them in person, we'll assume you are interested in the company and the position.

Tell him or her what are some of the aspects of the job description or company that intrigue you about the position. Do you like large, well-known companies and is this company one of them? Are you a fan of their products and a loyal customer?

Whatever it is, utilize your positive feelings when answering the question and, as always, keep in mind the other party. The employer has two interests in mind with this question:

1. They want to make sure the job they have to offer is the type of position you are pursuing.

2. They want to know, as the old saying goes, "What's in it for me?"

A sample response could be "Being a loyal customer with your brand, I am interested in working for a company such as yours that emphasizes quality products along with great customer service." (Compliments here and there throughout an interview are a great strategy, but don't overdo it). Continuing on, "I have spent much of the time in my present position working toward the highest level of customer service."

So the employer starts to feel comfortable that you would easily fit into his or her organization, you can follow-up with "I have researched your company and feel confident that it is the type of place I am looking for. The people I've spoken with seem happy and friendly and we share the same hard-working ethics."

4. "Where do you see yourself in 5-10 years?"

It's difficult to find good employees. Anyone who has ever had to conduct interviews and hire someone knows this. The interviewer doesn't want to hire someone only to find out that the person plans on moving to a far away state in the next year or that he is planning on changing careers soon. She wants to know that you will be around for awhile. That doesn't mean you need to insinuate you will still be with the company in 10 years, but you want to emphasize stability along with a desire to learn and grow.

"I would really like to settle down with a company that I can be proud of and continue to grow and learn. As long as I continue to be challenged, I would envision staying with your company for many years. I consider growth an important part of my career and I would like to take on additional responsibilities as the years go on. As my responsibilities increase, so does my opportunity to make an even greater, positive impact on this organization."

5. "What are your strengths and weaknesses?"

Here's the question everyone cringes when they hear it. No need to be afraid. Be honest and always have a positive twist to all answers. Let's start with your strengths. Since you read over the job description many times in order to prepare for the interview, you are an expert on the key words and qualifications the employer is looking for in their next employee. Utilize this knowledge when you answer the question.

If they are looking for an extremely organized person with great communication skills, discuss one or two examples of when you showed these skills. Maybe in your last job, you improved communication by writing weekly emails to key individuals in order to give them updates on major projects. Perhaps you spearheaded a project where you juggled multiple tasks and you not only organized yourself, but also the group as a whole.

Now onto the weaknesses. Everybody has something they can improve upon. Choose an aspect of your work life that you need to improve upon and position your response as "something to improve upon," not as a weakness—there is a difference. My favorite way of answering this question is like this: "I believe effective communication is a weakness for most individuals and companies as a whole. I can always improve upon my communications, both written and verbal. I set this as a goal last year and I'm happy to say that I am much better now that I have concentrated my efforts on achieving it."

You can go on to say "For example, over the past few months in my present position, I have set up a quick half hour weekly meeting with each of my staff members in order to discuss ongoing projects and also answer any questions he or she may have. Many mistakes happen because of lack of communication or miscommunication and both my employees and I have found these meetings to be extremely worthwhile."

You were honest with one of your weaknesses and you discuss what you have been doing about it. The key here is to make sure you ARE working on your weaknesses and have an example.

6. "Why should we hire you?"

"Why not?" is not the best answer to this question! Let's see what is a more appropriate response. As you did with your achievements on your resume, make sure you discuss specifics when answering this question. If the three major requirements of this job are:

- Increasing business partnerships

- Supervising a staff of four

- Managing a departmental budget

Address each point separately. "In my previous job, I was able to acquire five new clients in the first year." (Companies always love when employees can get up to speed quickly and start contributing FAST.) "Currently, I have a group of three programmers and one coordinator working in my group." Lastly, "My past two jobs have required me to create and manage an annual budget." Some other general statements you can make include: "I am a quick learner and can begin to add value to the company immediately."

7. "Do you have any questions?"

This is probably the last question the interviewer will ask you, so make sure you end with a bang. I urge you to prepare 4 to 6 questions before hand and write them on a notepad. You may think of other questions as you go through the interview, but at least you have a back up plan in case you don't.

Make sure you ask questions you really care about, don't just ask a question because that's what the experts tell you to do. This is your time to find out more information about this company. The company is interviewing you, but keep in mind that YOU are also interviewing the company.

Some good questions to ask are:

- What is the financial status of the company? Is it profitable? (Always good to get the broad picture of the company, so you don't make a mistake by signing on with a company that goes bankrupt in six months)

- Is this a new position or did someone leave this position? If someone left, why did they leave? Were they promoted or did they leave the company? (Good indicator of a few things: If the person was promoted, you now have positive evidence about the company's culture and how they treat and reward employees. If the person left, you can also understand a little more about the situation and why it happened)

- What do you like most about the company? What do you like least? And why? (This is always an interesting question, especially when you can ask it to several people at the company. This gives you a chance to compare answers and definitely see the weaknesses and strengths of a company)

- How would you describe your management style? (Especially good if the person you are interviewing with would be your direct supervisor)

- What traits are you looking for? (Most of the people you are speaking with did not directly contribute to the job posting description. It is always good to find out what certain individuals are looking for in their next hire)

About the Author: Paul Fontaine

Paul has extensive experience in marketing, public relations, advertising and publishing. His previous work experience has been with such well-known companies as Time-Life Books and The Franklin Mint. Paul has been published in various industry publications, both on and offline.

He has been giving career advice for over ten years. Paul has reviewed and critiqued hundreds of resumes and has helped create more effective communication tools to attract employer's attention and to find that perfect job. He has been on both sides of the desk as an interviewer and an interviewee.

Paul has studied in the U.S. and China. He received an undergraduate degree in Business Administration with an emphasis in Marketing and Communication from the University of Rhode Island. In addition, Paul has an M.B.A. from Villanova University in Pennsylvania.

Paul is President of Easy Online Guides, a business dedicated to creating and distributing high quality, easy-to-understand, how-to guides in an inexpensive and fast manner for online consumers.

You may contact Paul via email at **info@EasyOnlineGuides.com**.

0-595-24525-0

Printed in the United States
6902